# Seasonal Soups

# Seasonal Soups

LUCY SAUNDERS

CB
CONTEMPORARY
BOOKS
CHICAGO

**Library of Congress Cataloging-in-Publication Data**

Saunders, Lucy.
   Seasonal soups / Lucy Saunders.
      p.   cm.
   Includes index.
   ISBN 0-8092-4101-3 (paper)
   1. Soups. I. Title.
TX757   1991
641.8'13—dc20                                  91-20147
                                                   CIP

Published by Contemporary Books, Inc.
180 North Michigan Avenue, Chicago, Illinois 60601
Manufactured in the United States of America
International Standard Book Number: 0-8092-4101-3

To my grandmothers,
for letting me play in the kitchen,
and to my parents,
for encouraging me to work in the kitchen

# CONTENTS

# ACKNOWLEDGMENTS

Every book incurs debts of gratitude to be repaid with acknowledgment, though thanks alone sometimes seem insufficient to recognize the efforts of friends and colleagues! Thanks to my editor, Linda Gray, and my agent, Barry Bluestein, of Season to Taste Books, for their help in bringing the book to print.

I am grateful to the magazine and newspaper editors who have encouraged me over the years: Lisa Bertagnoli, Pam Erickson, Jack Kenny, Molly McQuade, Nancy Moore, Ron Tanner, and Ross Werland. Lee Wilkinson generously gave me the time needed at home to complete the text.

Thanks to Anne Swanson and Giles Schnierle for their help with the section on bases. I am indebted to Pam Adrien, Nancy Barocci, Carol Bartley, Jerry and Patti Bock, Cherrill Cregar, Ray Garcia, Meg Guthrie, Kristin Nelson, Arnie Pinkus, Sona Rejebian, Banlu Vitayaudom, and Trina Wellman for sharing their recipes. Thanks to Leslie Graham and Jan Longone for sharing their research and libraries. Special thanks to Alex Panozzo and Susan Witz of the Heartland Spa for sharing their expertise in diet and healthful soups.

The inverse of the proverb "too many cooks spoil the broth" is "many testers improve the soup." My stockpot floweth over with thanks to everyone who tested or tasted the recipes in development: Marietta Abrams, Allyson Buckley, Doug and Lydia Chene,

Kathy Dickus, Peter Gardner, Vicki Holmes, John Kehlen, Tracy Koe, Mary Jo Peer, Bob Schaffer, Barb Schechtman, Chris Soderquist, Chris and John Thale, Kathrin Theis, Fred Wagner, and especially Erin Vang, who tested Lamb and Barley Soup on a sizzling summer day when the thermometer reached 110°F.

Love and gratitude to Elise; to Tom, Jack, and Mary, for all six burners and more; to my family, Sally and Bill, Margery, Tony and Kristin; and to my grandmother, Phyllis Leatherbee Woodruff, for her example.

# INTRODUCTION:
## SOUP IN SEASON

"Soup puts the heart at ease, calms the violence of hunger, eliminates the tensions of the day, and awakens and refines the appetite."
— French chef Auguste Escoffier

Let March winds blow and April showers fall, as long as we can chase away the chills with a warming bowl of soup. When summer's heat makes sidewalks sizzle, a chilled fruit soup is a wonderful cooler. Fall's abundant harvest offers a colorful array of produce ripe for creating bountiful autumn soups. Falling temperatures and a first snow are winter's hints that steaming kettles of stews and hearty soups will soon be tasted. Soup nourishes both body and soul year-round.

Ideally, soups start with the most intensely flavored raw foods available, since adding water or stock will invariably dilute their flavor. That means cooking with seasonal fruits and vegetables at their peak. *Seasonal Soups* takes advantage of in-season produce, meats, and seafood to yield more than 80 delightful—and healthful—recipes.

Many of the recipes offer time-saving and calorie-reducing tips for cooks who must watch the clock or the scales. Most are simple enough to be made in less than an hour. Like many things in life, however, soup improves with age. Flavors mingle as the stock

1

absorbs the seasonings and ingredients. Always try to make soup a few hours, or even a few days, before serving it. The extra planning will result in extra-flavorful soups.

Soup accommodates the cook; add lots of rich ingredients to make it a meal or only a few light herbs to make it a low-cal first course. Simple soups made of pureed vegetables with herbs, such as Basil Tomato Potato Soup, make easy and quick suppers. More elaborate dishes, such as Tata Marie's Mussel Soup, are ideal for entertaining.

Few dishes are as easy for the beginning cook to prepare as soup. If you can boil water, you've mastered the first step. Soup is very forgiving: improvisation in the soup pot can yield tasty results. As you experiment, you'll realize that it's easy to produce a stunning soup without lots of work.

## FREEZING AND THAWING SOUPS

Only a few soups, such as vichyssoise and bouillabaisse, are harmed by freezing. The rule of thumb is: do not freeze dairy-based cream or cheese soups, soups containing seafood in the shell, or delicately seasoned soups. Everything else may be frozen. That's because the soup is rarely affected by the slight addition of water formed in freezing and thawing.

If I know that part of my batch of soup is destined for the freezer, I will deliberately undercook the freezer portion of the soup by 15 minutes or so. The crispier vegetables withstand freezing and thawing better than well-cooked ones, which can become mushy.

Try not to freeze soups made with canned or frozen ingredients, because they will lose too much texture and flavor.

Soups fare best when slowly thawed in the refrigerator overnight. (However, in a pinch, I've thrown a block of frozen broth-based vegetable soup in a pot with ½ cup of boiling water and melted the soup for dinner.) All you need to do is reheat the soup slowly and let it reduce a bit to regain its original thickness. You can also add a thickener, such as potato starch, arrowroot, cornstarch, or pureed cooked vegetables, to a thawed and thin soup. Taste the reheated soup and add more seasonings if necessary to restore its vibrant flavor.

2

Avoid thawing and reheating more soup than you will eat at one sitting, because soup does not improve with constant freezing and reheating. Instead, stock up on resealable plastic containers that will let you freeze soups in exact 8- or 10-ounce portions. An assortment of single servings of soups is also much more convenient for the late-night diner foraging in the freezer for something to eat.

## MICROWAVE CONSIDERATIONS

Few soups benefit from cooking in a microwave oven—at least not the first time around. Make your soups on the stovetop and let them simmer slowly. Then, hold them for a few hours before serving to let the flavors meld. Precooked soups, however, can be reheated in the microwave, especially clear broth-based soups.

Thick, creamy soups and stews pose a special problem in the microwave: they often erupt in explosive splatters, making a mess of the oven. Cover the dish with a plate or paper towel to contain the splatters. Stop the microwave two or three times while reheating the soup and stir it. It will reheat evenly, without scorching.

Let a microwave-heated soup sit a bit; then stir it well before taking your first mouthful. Sometimes, the center of the soup can be scalding while the surface merely is warm. This is an especially important precaution to take when giving microwave-heated soups to children.

I do not recommend reheating cheese soups in the microwave, as they often curdle. If a slightly grainy texture does not bother you, though, the microwave will suffice for the chore of reheating a dairy-based or cream soup—without dirtying a pan.

## SUBSTITUTIONS FOR YOUR HEALTH

Many of the recipes in this book use vegetables and fruits that are rich in vitamins and abundant sources of natural fiber. However, a few of the recipes do call for cream, butter, and other fats. If you prefer lower-fat soups, try the following substitutions:

▷ Start with a vegetable-based or wine broth instead of meat stock or use only chilled and defatted meat stock.

3

▷ Add nonfat dry milk instead of whole milk, cream, or half-and-half. Add 2 tablespoons more of the powdered milk and 1 tablespoon less of water to create a creamier blend. Add to soup by first dissolving the powdered milk in a little warm stock or broth in a blender and then returning the mixture to the pot.

▷ Nonfat farmer cheese, hoop cheese, nonfat skim cottage cheese, or dry baker's cheese may be pureed with a little stock or broth and added to the soup instead of cream.

▷ Use evaporated nonfat/skim milk instead of cream.

▷ Use olive oil or vegetable oil instead of butter.

▷ Use low-fat cheeses made from skim milk instead of regular cheddar and Parmesan cheeses.

To meet guidelines for sodium-restricted diets, do not add salt to the soups. Instead:

▷ Try using extra pepper, a dash of bitters, or a squeeze of a fresh lemon wedge to add flavor to soups.

▷ Chop a handful of fresh herbs and sprinkle on top of the soup as a garnish.

▷ Just a few grains of celery salt or no-salt seasoning blends added at the table can impart flavor to the soup without adding lots of sodium.

▷ Horseradish or dry mustard can add flavor, too.

## SERVING SOUPS

What should you serve with a bowl of soup?

First on almost everyone's list is some kind of bread. The historical precedent for this dates from Elizabethan times, when soup was called "sop," after the pieces of bread used to mop up drippings, broths, and other cooking juices. Guests could read their host's generosity or stinginess by counting the pieces of bread served in the soup.

Many people still enjoy eating soup as a "sop," dunking pieces of crusty whole-grain bread into a hot broth, and I can think of no better complement to a bowl of soup. On the other hand, you would look stingy, by modern as well as Elizabethan standards, if all you served for lunch was a bowl of soup with a few pieces of bread!

Of course, the type of meal you are planning should dictate the accompaniments to soup. An elegant, five-course meal, for example, should be prefaced with a soup light enough not to spoil your guests' appetites for what is to follow.

In her *Good Food Book*, Jane Brody said she often eats soup, with several pieces of bread and fruit, for breakfast. More typical is to have a bowl of soup for lunch, with a half-sandwich or bread and a salad or perhaps some fruit. The textural contrast of the soup, a crunchy salad, and chewy bread makes the meal all the more pleasurable.

A dinner soup may be a meal in a bowl, such as Slow-Fire Chili or Lobster Catchers' Seafood Chowder. When you're choosing a soup to precede other dinner courses, pay attention to the elements of taste, color, and texture. If you will have baked tomatoes with your entree, avoid serving tomato soup. Likewise, if your entree will be served with a heavy cream sauce, choose a clear, zesty soup for the first course.

## PRESENTATION

"Beautiful soup, so rich and green,
Waiting in a hot tureen!"
Lewis Carroll, *Alice's Adventures in Wonderland*

Tureens may make fine centerpieces for formal entertaining, but few families use them for everyday dining. Most of us serve soup straight from the pot and carry it to the table in individual bowls.

The unfortunate effect of such convenience is that the soup becomes tepid or cools entirely en route to the table.

Avoid this by warming soup bowls before filling them. To warm microwavable dishes, simply pour ½ cup of water into each soup bowl and microwave it on high power for 2 minutes. Use an oven mitt or towel to remove the heated dish from the microwave. Then pour out the hot water, wipe the bowl dry, and fill the still-warm bowl. If you're using fragile or nonmicrowavable china, run warm water into the bowl and gradually increase the tap temperature to hot. Then dry the bowl and fill it with hot soup.

Some of my favorite serving dishes aren't even made of china. Soups can be served in individual "bowls" of hollowed-out melon halves, pumpkins, or squash. My cousin Kathrin even presents her favorite Thanksgiving soup in a "tureen" made from a turban squash. Again, preheat the container by filling it with boiling water. For cold soups, you'll want to chill containers. Just place them in the refrigerator until they are cold.

# GARNITURE

Legend has it that consommé was invented at the behest of King Louis IV who requested a clear soup in which he could behold his royal visage while he dined.

Most of us would rather savor an excellent garnish for our soup than worry about spoiling the view of our visages. Making a soup look good means more than just serving it in a pretty dish. An appealing garnish brings out color and flavor and adds texture. Even small amounts of leftovers can be recycled as garnishes to great effect. A small portion of leftover omelet, for example, can be chopped with parsley and fresh bell pepper to make a great garnish for a bean soup.

Here is a list of potential garnishes:

### CHOPPED FRESH HERBS

| | |
|---|---|
| Celery leaves | Paprika |
| Chives | Parsley |
| Dill | Rosemary |
| Lemon verbena | Sorrel |
| Mint | Watercress |

### DICED COOKED MEATS

| | |
|---|---|
| Bacon | Prosciutto |
| Canadian bacon | Spicy sausages, such as kiel- |
| Chicken | basa |
| Ham | Liver |
| Turkey | |

### FRUITS

| | |
|---|---|
| Avocado | Mandarin oranges |
| Melon balls | Thin slices of citrus |
| Lemon zest | Sliced apples or pears |

## BREAD AND STARCHES

Toasted pita strips (see Index)
Cooked pasta
Crispy tortilla strips
Cooked rice
Seasoned croutons

Browned diced potatoes
Slices of toasted bread with cheese
Ricotta-Dill Dumplings (see Index)

## DAIRY PRODUCTS

Whipped cream
Sliced or chopped hard-cooked eggs

Grated Parmesan cheese
Yogurt
Sour cream

# 1
# THE WELL-STOCKED STOCKPOT
❧ ❧

Stocks are the building blocks for most soups, yet many people avoid making them, feeling it's just too much work. Though stocks made from scratch do require planning, they demand very little labor.

The key is to have the right tools on hand. You'll need ingredients such as meat or poultry bones, vegetables, herbs, and seasonings and tools such as a large stockpot, a slotted spoon or a colander, and a skimmer (see page 10).

My grandmother saves bones left over from roast chicken or beef, along with the chilled pan juices from these meats. (A butcher probably will save bones for you, too, if you ask ahead.) She also keeps scraps of carrot, celery, and onion (including skins) in a resealable plastic bag in the freezer. When she has a full bag, it's time to make stock. Her example is easy to follow, especially if you cook lots of vegetables or often make salads.

In general, I add only carrot, celery, and onion to meat stocks. Some vegetables, such as radishes, cucumbers, and cruciferous vegetables such as cabbages and broccoli, are too strong-flavored for my taste. However, many cooks do use a wider range of vegetables in making stocks. Chef Alex Panozzo of the Heartland Spa uses leeks, turnips, parsnips, and other intensely flavored vegetables. Use what you personally find appealing.

Some professional chefs use vegetables that have gone beyond ripe to overripe. Others disdain using anything but the finest and freshest ingredients. I find that stocks are remarkably forgiving. Limp celery, soft carrots, and slightly sprouted onions get tossed into my stockpot. Since these vegetables will later be discarded or pureed, I don't care if they are blemished. However, I do not use any ingredients that are slimy, moldy, or smell of decay. Economy can be pushed too far!

When you're making stock, be sure to use a nonreactive stainless-steel or enameled pot to avoid metallic tastes. You may also use a pressure cooker. Just be sure to fill it no more than half full, as the foam from the boiling stock may clog the vents.

The steps to making stocks are easy: simply brown the bones (if making beef, veal or pork stocks), add the bones to boiling water with seasonings and vegetables, reduce the heat to let the stock simmer, and cook until the water reduces by one-third to one-half, depending on the desired strength of the stock.

Some people like to add spices to their stocks in the form of a bouquet garni, a cheesecloth bundle that holds one bay leaf, two sprigs each of fresh thyme and parsley, and three or four whole peppercorns. If making little bundles of spices is not your bag, just add the loose spices to the stock. Strain them out when you pour the stock through a cheesecloth-lined sieve or colander.

Use a skimmer to remove any foam that comes to the surface as the stock boils. After the stock reduces, strain it through a cheesecloth-lined colander and puree the cooked vegetables. They will have lost all their flavor but can be saved to use as a soup thickener in lieu of roux (a blend of butter or fat cooked with flour).

At this point you may want to clarify the stock. Some cooks swear by the method of clarifying stock with a beaten egg; my method is just as simple. Chill it overnight; the next day, lift off congealed fats and ladle out the cold stock, which may have a jellied consistency. Impurities settle to the bottom of the pot, so you can toss them out.

If you want to defat a stock but don't have time to chill it, blot the oily surface with heavy paper towels to soak up the fat. Use a pair of tongs to lift the paper towel off the surface of the hot stock.

Given the need for planning when making stock, I try to make enough for two or three batches of soup at a time, freezing the chilled stock in 1-quart or 1-gallon resealable plastic bags. If the seals are leakproof, the bags may be laid flat on the freezer shelves to take up less room.

You might also try making a few gallons of stock and slowly simmering it for 5 to 6 hours to reduce it to a concentrate. The concentrate may be frozen (for 4 to 6 months) in less space than regular stock. Some cooks even freeze concentrated stock in ice cube trays to use for sauces. Just be sure to dilute it before use.

Stock is highly perishable and should be frozen if you do not plan to use it right away. One word of caution: what you gain in convenience you may lose in flavor. Over time, stock that has been frozen loses its fresh taste. You may need to adjust seasonings and add fresh ingredients to perk up a long-frozen stock. A teaspoon of lemon juice or herb vinegar can work wonders.

## TOOLS FOR MAKING STOCK

Have these essential items on hand when you make a stock.

1 heavy skillet, 12 or more inches in diameter, to brown bones *or* 1 rimmed heavy-duty baking pan to hold bones during oven browning

Measuring cups or pitchers to pour water into stockpot

1 stockpot, at least 6 quarts in size, preferably a 2- or 3-gallon stockpot made of non-reactive stainless steel or enameled metal, with lid

1 3-quart soup pot (although a range of pot sizes, from 2 quarts to 2 gallons, gives you the most flexibility)

1 large colander (or a large chinoise, a professional chef's fine-mesh sieve shaped like a funnel)

Cheesecloth, to line the colander or to make bouquets garnis

1 ladle, to pour out stock for single servings

1 food mill or blender or food processor, to puree cooked vegetables (a food mill with interchangeable disks gives greater control over consistency of the puree than does a food processor)

1 skimmer, slotted spoon, or flat wire-mesh spoon to remove foam from boiling stock

You may also want to have:

1 pressure cooker, at least 6 quarts in size, to make fast broths and cook beans for soups

Tongs, to lift out bones and bouquets garnis from hot stock

## USING CANNED STOCKS AND BROTHS

Feel free to use canned stocks in making any of the recipes in this book. I recommend low-sodium broths, because the regular varieties can contain as much as 750-1,000 milligrams of sodium per cup. Low-sodium varieties have just 100-250 milligrams of sodium per cup. Taste the canned broth to test its strength—some broths benefit from an extra ½ cup of water or milk to dilute the strong flavor.

## BASE ALTERNATIVES

Soups can be made in a matter of minutes if you have stocks on hand. For time-pressed cooks, an alternative to homemade stock is the base, or concentrated canned essence of meats and vegetables.

I was skeptical about the flavor of bases until I sampled several new varieties that are low in sodium and contain only natural ingredients. Far from the artificial Day-Glo yellow chicken bases I had seen in cooking schools in the 1970s, the new batches of bases look—and taste—surprisingly like the real thing.

Best of all, bases require a fraction of the storage space of stocks. A gallon of stock may be made from several teaspoons of concentrate in only a minute and exactly when needed. That frees the soup cook from planning and space constraints.

Reconstitute a base according to the manufacturer's instructions, taste it, and dilute a little more if necessary. Be sure to taste the base mix to see if it is salty; if so, do not salt the soup again until served.

Brands of bases popular with professional chefs include The Gourmet Edge, Eatem Low-Sodium bases, Minor's, and Perfect Addition. They are available at specialty food shops or see the appendix for mail-order sources.

# CHICKEN STOCK

*I prefer to use a big old bird and only onions, carrots, celery, and a bouquet garni for flavorings. You can also make turkey stock with this recipe by using 5–6 pounds of turkey necks or wings or leftovers from a roasted bird, with its pan drippings. Be sure to substitute sage for thyme in the bouquet garni to bring out the turkey flavor.*

Makes 2 quarts

3 tablespoons vegetable oil
1 6- to 8-pound stewing
  chicken, cut up (giblets
  removed)
2 medium-sized white or yellow
  onions, unpeeled
2 large carrots, trimmed and
  scrubbed
3 large ribs celery, including
  leaves
1 gallon water (or more, to
  cover chicken)

BOUQUET GARNI:
1 bay leaf
1 sprig fresh thyme *or* 1
  teaspoon dried thyme
2 cloves garlic
3 peppercorns
1 5-inch square of cheesecloth

1 Place oil in a heavy 2-gallon stockpot over medium-high heat. Add chicken, one or two pieces at a time to avoid crowding the pot, and brown until golden. Once all the parts are browned, place them all back in the pot with the vegetables and water. Bundle spices for the bouquet garni in cheesecloth and tie in a knot to secure. Add bouquet garni to pot.

2 Bring stock to a boil and skim off the foam. Reduce heat and simmer, uncovered, for 2 hours or until chicken meat falls off bones when nudged with a fork. The water will have reduced by about half; if more has boiled away, add a little water.

3 Strain stock through a large colander, discarding bouquet garni and vegetables. Remove skin from chicken and chop meat; it may be added to a soup later.

4 Chill stock and remove fat that congeals on top. Divide the chilled stock among 2-cup freezer containers and freeze for up to 3 to 4 months or refrigerate and use within 3 days.

# VERY BROWN BEEF STOCK

*Well-browned bones give this stock a pleasantly dark hue. You may wish to use the pan drippings from a roast beef instead of oil to brown the bones. The dark juices will add color, too.*

Makes 2 quarts

4 pounds beef bones, with
  meat
3 tablespoons vegetable oil
2 medium-sized white or yellow
  onions, unpeeled
2 large carrots, trimmed and
  scrubbed
3 large ribs celery, including
  leaves
1 gallon water

BOUQUET GARNI:
1 bay leaf
1 sprig fresh thyme *or* 1
  teaspoon dried thyme
3 cloves
3 peppercorns
1 5-inch square of cheesecloth

1. Preheat oven to 475°F. Rub bones with oil and place in a heavy roasting pan. Brown in the oven for 20–30 minutes, turning once, until deep golden brown. Place bones in a heavy 2-gallon stockpot with vegetables and water. Bundle spices for bouquet garni in cheesecloth and tie in a knot to secure. Add bouquet garni to pot.

2. Bring stock to a boil and skim off foam. Reduce heat and simmer, uncovered, for 2 hours or until stock is reduced by almost one-half.

3. Strain stock through a large colander and discard bones, bouquet garni, and vegetables.

4. Chill stock and remove fat that congeals on top. Divide chilled stock among 2-cup freezer containers and freeze for up to 3 to 4 months or refrigerate and use within 3 days.

# SPICY PORK STOCK

*This makes a great stock for legume and pea soups or purees of cruciferous veggies.*

Makes 2 quarts

> 3-4 pounds pork neck bones
> 2 tablespoons vegetable oil
> 1 gallon water
> 2 tablespoons pickling spices
> 1 large yellow onion, chopped
> 2 medium-sized carrots,
>   chopped
> 2 large ribs celery, chopped

1. Brown bones in oil in a heavy 2-gallon stockpot over high heat. When seared, add the water, spices, and vegetables.

2. Bring stock to a boil and skim off foam. Reduce heat and simmer, uncovered, for 2 hours or until stock is reduced by almost one-half.

3. Strain stock through a large colander and discard bones and vegetables.

4. Chill stock and remove fat that congeals on top. Divide chilled stock among 2-cup freezer containers and freeze for up to 3 to 4 months or refrigerate and use within 3 days.

# GOLDEN GARLIC BROTH

*Vegetarians are always looking for stocks that have the same golden color as a chicken or beef broth for clear soups. The caramelized garlic cloves give this broth a lovely golden color, while the taste of the brown sugar is barely noticeable. Substitute it for meat stocks if you want a low-cal soup.*

Makes 1½ quarts

> 6 whole heads garlic (about
>   50-60 cloves)
> 3 tablespoons vegetable oil
> 1 tablespoon light brown
>   sugar, packed
> 2½ quarts water
> Salt and freshly ground pepper
>   to taste

1. Preheat oven to 350°F. Separate heads of garlic and remove papery skins; leave each clove whole.

2. In a deep roasting pan, mix vegetable oil and brown sugar. Toss garlic in the sugar and oil and bake for 10-15 minutes. Stir cloves often, until garlic is lightly and evenly browned (do not burn).

3. Remove pan from oven and scrape contents into a stockpot. Cover with water and bring to simmer over low heat. Simmer for 1 hour or until garlic is soft and stock is a golden color.

4. Strain stock through a colander, season with salt and pepper, and chill in a tightly sealed container. This stock will keep in the refrigerator for up to 1 month or may be kept frozen for up to 4 to 6 months.

# POTATO BROTH

*If you have no soup bones for a meat stock, this is a good last-minute substitute. It may also be used instead of meat stock for vegetarian diets.*

Makes 2 quarts

3-4 tablespoons vegetable oil
4 large Idaho or baking
    potatoes (3-4 pounds total),
    scrubbed with skins on and
    chopped coarse
2 medium-sized yellow onions,
    unpeeled
2 large carrots, trimmed and
    scrubbed
3 large ribs celery, including
    leaves
2½ quarts water

BOUQUET GARNI:
1 bay leaf
3 sprigs fresh parsley
2 cloves garlic
6 peppercorns
1 5-inch square of cheesecloth

1 Place oil in a heavy 2-gallon stockpot over medium-high heat. Add potatoes and brown until crisp. Add vegetables and water. Bundle spices for bouquet garni inside cheesecloth and tie in a knot to secure. Add bouquet garni to pot and bring stock to a boil.

2 Reduce heat to medium-low and simmer stock, uncovered, for 1 hour.

3 Strain stock through a large colander and discard bouquet garni and vegetables.

4 Chill stock. Divide chilled stock among 2-cup freezer containers and freeze for up to 4 to 6 months or refrigerate and use within 3 days.

# CREAMY RICE BROTH

*Vegetarians who do not eat dairy products often find it difficult to duplicate the creamy look of a soup made with roux and milk. A puree of rice, cooked with seasoned water, makes a good substitute.*

Makes 1½ quarts

3 tablespoons vegetable oil
2 cups Japanese short-grain
    rice
2 medium-sized yellow onions,
    unpeeled
2 medium carrots, trimmed
    and scrubbed
3 medium ribs celery,
    including leaves
2½ quarts water

BOUQUET GARNI:
1 bay leaf
3 sprigs fresh parsley
1 teaspoon dried thyme
2 cloves garlic
3 peppercorns
1 5-inch square of cheesecloth

1. Place oil in a heavy 2-gallon stockpot over medium-high heat. Add rice and sauté for 5-8 minutes, stirring often. Add vegetables and water. Bundle spices for bouquet garni inside cheesecloth and tie in a knot to secure. Add bouquet garni to pot.

2. Bring stock to a simmer and cook, covered, for 1 hour.

3. Using a slotted spoon, lift bouquet garni and vegetables out of stock and discard them.

4. Cool stock and puree it in a blender. Divide chilled stock among 2-cup containers and freeze for up to 4 to 6 months or refrigerate and use within 3 days.

# VEGETABLE STOCK

*Alex Panozzo, chef of the Heartland Spa in Gilman, Illinois, makes a vegetarian stock as the base for all the low-calorie soups served at the spa. He uses carrots, leeks, celery, turnips, mushroom stems, scallions, and even the yellow skins and ends of onions—all trimmings from vegetables used to prepare other dishes. Avoid vegetables that have been sprayed or waxed, cucumbers, radishes, potato skins, bitter greens, and cruciferous vegetables, since they impart an "off" flavor to the stock. Just place scraps in a resealable container in the freezer until you have collected the 5–6 cups necessary to make 1 quart of stock.*

5–6 cups mixed vegetable
   trimmings (from carrots,
   celery, leeks, mushrooms,
   onions, scallions, turnips,
   potatoes)
6–7 cups water

BOUQUET GARNI:
1 bay leaf
3 sprigs fresh parsley
1 teaspoon dried thyme
3 cloves garlic
6 peppercorns
1 5-inch square of cheesecloth

1 Place vegetable trimmings in a 2-gallon stockpot and cover with water. Bundle spices for bouquet garni inside cheesecloth and tie in a knot to secure. Add bouquet garni to pot. Turn up heat, bring stock to a full boil, and then reduce to a simmer.

2 Cook for about 1 hour, skimming off foam if necessary. Strain the broth. This stock keeps refrigerated for up to 3 weeks or frozen for up to 4 to 6 months.

# VERY BROWN VEAL STOCK

Makes 1 gallon

7 pounds veal shank and neck
  bones
2 tablespoons olive oil
2 cups peeled and sliced
  carrot
2 cups peeled and sliced
  yellow onion
1 leek, well washed and
  chopped
2 cups good-quality dry white
  wine
1 tablespoon salt
6 quarts water

BOUQUET GARNI:
1 bay leaf
3 sprigs fresh parsley
1 teaspoon dried thyme
2 cloves garlic
3 peppercorns
1 5-inch square of cheesecloth

1. Preheat oven to 500°F. Wash bones and pat dry. Place bones on a baking sheet and bake for 20-30 minutes or until bones are browned.

2. Heat oil in a large stockpot. Add carrots, onions, and leek and sauté over medium-high heat 5-8 minutes. Add browned bones and any pan juices to the sautéed vegetables.

3. Add wine and salt and cook until liquid is reduced to a syrupy consistency. Add water. Bundle spices for bouquet garni inside cheesecloth and tie in a knot to secure. Add bouquet garni to pot, bring stock to a boil, and skim off foam.

4. Reduce heat and simmer, partially covered, for several hours or until broth is thickened and meat is falling off bones. Strain through a colander and discard bones, vegetables, and bouquet garni. Store stock in freezer for up to 3 months or refrigerate and use within 3 days.

# FISH STOCK

*Be sure to save the trimmings and any leftover fillets from a fresh catch for this stock. Otherwise, call your fish purveyors and ask them to save some bones and heads for you. Try to get salmon, trout, or snapper bones for a light, delicate stock. Oily fish, such as bluefish, can be too strong-flavored for a fish soup that uses white-fleshed fillets.*

Makes 1½ quarts

4 pounds fish heads and
   bones, rinsed
1 cup peeled and chopped
   yellow onion
½ cup sliced carrot
½ cup sliced celery

2 teaspoons fresh *or* 1
   teaspoon dried thyme
1 bay leaf
1 teaspoon freshly ground
   white pepper
2½ quarts

1. Place fish, onion, carrot, celery, thyme, bay leaf, pepper, and water in a 1-gallon nonreactive stockpot. Bring to a boil over medium heat and skim off foam.

2. Reduce heat to low and simmer, uncovered, for 1 hour. Remove from heat and strain through a colander, discarding solids.

3. Chill and strain again, this time through a cheesecloth-lined colander, to clarify the stock. Keeps refrigerated for 1-2 days or frozen for up to 1 month.

# 2
# SPRING

❧ ❧

Perhaps the most reliable indication that spring is on its way is the selection of produce available at the market. Tender, thin asparagus, small snap peas, baby lettuce, new potatoes, sweet Vidalia onions, and other vegetables are, to me, the real harbingers of spring. Fresh herbs also begin to appear, augmenting the lone bunches of parsley that are the mainstay of winter kitchens.

Vegetables in season include artichokes, avocados, green bell peppers, radishes, and watercress. Cruciferous vegetables, such as cabbages, cauliflower, brussels sprouts, Swiss chard, and kohlrabi, are also available. Late spring brings Vidalia onions and shallots. Small, fat bunches of spinach are sold almost everywhere by May, as are tiny red and white potatoes.

Spring meats such as lamb and young pork offer good values. (The famed "spring baby lamb" found in European markets is hard to find here, but the tradition of eating this delicacy in the spring lingers.) Crawfish for gumbo are available by mail order from Louisiana beginning in late April or early May. Many of the saltwater fish recommended for the Bahamas Fish Chowder are available at this time, as are Atlantic mussels.

Spring fruits and berries are juicy and sweet in their prime. Look at their color and inhale their intense aroma. Unlike the often perfectly colored but tasteless winter look-alikes, spring berries are redolent with fragrance and flavor. Do wait until late spring for locally grown strawberries to make the Strawberry Soup. They will be lush, juicy, and red throughout, quite unlike the hybrid berries, with their tough white cores, that are sold in the winter.

Spring brings forth a delicious, colorful array of nature's best soup ingredients. Make the most of the variety of fruits and vegetables available by making several batches of soups or cooked purees and freezing them for later use.

# LEMON ARTICHOKE SOUP

*This soup—a variation on avgolemono, or Greek egg-lemon soup—contains slivered artichoke hearts for a slightly different taste. Accompanied by a tomato-cucumber-olive salad and fresh, crusty bread, it makes a savory, satisfying lunch.*

Serves 4

> 3 tablespoons long-grain white rice
> 1 quart chicken stock (see Index)
> 2 boiled artichokes trimmed of all leaves, bottoms and stems chopped
> 2 large eggs
> Juice of 1 lemon (4-5 tablespoons), or more to taste
> Salt and freshly ground pepper to taste

1. Simmer rice in broth in a 2-quart enameled saucepan until rice is soft, about 20 minutes.

2. Cut artichoke hearts into 1-inch slivers and add to broth.

3. In a medium-size glass or enameled bowl, beat eggs and lemon juice until fluffy. Add ⅓ cup of hot broth to egg, two tablespoons at a time, whisking after each addition as if to make a custard. When egg mixture is warm and yellow, pour it into hot soup, whisking well. The soup should be thickened and light yellow. Taste and add more lemon juice if desired. Add salt and pepper and serve hot.

# CHINESE EGG FLOWER SOUP

*This qualifies as a diet soup suitable for light lunches designed to shed excess winter weight. A 6-ounce portion has just 75 calories! Miso is used in many Asian soups; it is the equivalent of a soup base, made from soy or rice instead of meat products. It is sold in jars or packets in the Oriental food sections of many markets or by mail order (see Appendix). Miso can be very salty, so be sure to choose a low-sodium variety.*

Serves 4

2 cups chicken stock (see Index)
2 cups reconstituted low-sodium miso broth
⅓ cup thinly sliced fresh shiitake mushrooms
3 tablespoons minced scallion
2 large egg whites

1 tablespoon rice flour (see Note)
2 teaspoons water
1 teaspoon oyster sauce (see Note)
Chinese crispy rice noodles, crushed, or chow mein noodles for garnish

☐1 Combine chicken stock and miso broth in a 2-quart soup pot. Bring to a simmer. Add mushrooms and scallions and simmer for 10 minutes more; then reduce heat to low.

☐2 In a measuring cup, whisk together egg whites, rice flour, and water until well blended.

☐3 Pour egg white mixture into soup pot using a circular motion, making sure not to stir the soup until egg whites have set.

☐4 Add oyster sauce to soup and stir, breaking strands of egg white into flowery noodles. Garnish with a sprinkling of crushed Chinese crispy noodles and serve immediately.

*Note: Rice flour and oyster sauce are available in the Oriental section of many supermarkets, as well as in Asian grocery stores.*

# AVOCADO CREAM WITH CRAB FLAKES

*Use the ripest avocados you can find at the market—they will have the best flavor! I use the dark green Haas variety, which to me seem richer in taste, although you can use the light green Fuerte avocados too.*

Serves 4

> 2 cups chicken stock (see Index)
> 1 cup dry white wine
> ½ teaspoon celery salt
> 3 medium-sized ripe avocados (about 1¼ cups pulp)
> ¼ cup fresh lemon juice
> ¾ cup cooked and flaked crabmeat, canned or frozen with all shell bits removed
> Cumin Toasts (recipe follows) for garnish

1. Mix stock and wine in a medium saucepan and set over medium heat. Add celery salt.

2. Peel and pit avocados. Chop and place in a blender. Add 3 to 4 tablespoons of warm stock and the lemon juice to avocados. Blend on high speed until smooth. Return mixture to pot and stir well.

3. Add crabmeat. Heat thoroughly and garnish with Cumin Toasts. Serve hot.

# CUMIN TOASTS

2 slices extra-thin white bread
2 tablespoons olive oil
2 teaspoons ground cumin

[1] Brush both sides of each slice of bread with oil. Sprinkle ½ teaspoon cumin on one side of each slice.

[2] Heat an ungreased nonstick skillet over medium heat. Place bread in the skillet, cumin side down, and toast until that side is lightly browned, about 2 minutes. Sprinkle ½ teaspoon cumin on the top side of each slice. Flip bread over and toast for another 2 minutes.

[3] Remove bread from skillet and cut into squares (sized according to your taste and the size of your serving dishes).

# BANJAR ABOUR

*The thick, porridge texture of this soup is accented with hints of mint. A good friend, Sona Rejebian, makes this spinach soup as soon as fresh young bunches of spinach appear in the markets. It is an old Armenian recipe, given to Sona by her aunt, Satenig Ketchoyian.*

Serves 6

1 cup pressed barley (see
   Note)
1 quart water
1½ cups washed, trimmed, and
   chopped fresh spinach
2 tablespoons unsalted butter
   or margarine
1 cup chopped sweet Vidalia
   onion
2 teaspoons dried mint *or* 2
   tablespoons fresh mint

1 large egg, beaten
1 tablespoon all-purpose flour
2 cups plain nonfat yogurt
2 cups buttermilk
Salt and freshly ground pepper
   to taste
2-3 tablespoons milk if
   needed

1. Rinse barley. Place in a 3-quart pot, cover with water, and bring to a boil. Reduce heat and simmer, covered, for 45 minutes or until barley is tender and all the water has been absorbed. Add spinach during the last 15 minutes of cooking.

2. While the barley cooks, heat butter in a medium-sized skillet, add onion, and sauté over low heat until translucent. Remove from heat and add mint. Set aside.

3. Beat egg and flour together in a large bowl. Add yogurt and beat until smooth. Mix in buttermilk.

4. Pour yogurt mixture over cooked barley-spinach mixture and blend. Heat until just simmering; then add onion and mint and stir well. Add salt and pepper.

5. If the soup is too thick for your taste, thin with 2-3 tablespoons milk. Serve in warmed bowls.

*Note: Dzedzadz, or pressed barley, is available at many Oriental and Middle Eastern markets. It has the advantage of cooking faster than regular pearled barley. You may substitute regular barley, if you prefer, but you'll need to extend the cooking time by 15–20 minutes, or as per package directions.*

# TATA MARIE'S MUSSEL SOUP

❧ ❧

*My friend Marietta nicknamed her French aunt (tante) "Tata";
this is an adaptation of her aunt's Algerian recipe for spring-
time mussel soup. Mussels are high in protein and one of the
less expensive varieties of shellfish when in season. Though
farm-raised mussels are available year-round, their texture is
often less firm and their flavor less pronounced than "wild"
mussels.*

*Plan to spend at least 15 minutes scrubbing the shells free of
beards (the long black strands that bewhisker the shells) and
barnacles. I suggest rinsing the mussels twice before tackling
them with a stiff-bristled brush or even clean steel wool pads
(not the soapy kind but the ones you'll find at the hardware
store).*

*Place the mussels in a large bowl. Cover them with water and
sprinkle with 1 tablespoon of flour. The live mussels will open
their shells to eat the flour, making it easier to rinse away grit
from inside the shells. Rinse again with plain water and drain.
Use your fingernails (or a pair of needle-nose pliers to save your
manicure) to pull off the beards and scrape away any barnacles. Thoroughly rinse again after scrubbing, and you'll have
mussels full of flavor and free of grit.*

*Live mussels will clamp shut when tapped gently on the
shell and will open after cooking. Be sure to discard any mussels that do not open after cooking as they will not be fresh.*

Serves 4

3 tablespoons olive oil
1 tablespoon minced garlic
1 cup chopped sweet Vidalia
  or Walla Walla onion
1 cup chopped red bell pepper
2 cups seeded and chopped
  fresh tomato
¼ cup chopped fresh parsley
½ cup pitted and chopped
  black Mediterranean olives

¼ cup fresh lemon juice
½ teaspoon crumbled saffron
  threads
2 cups dry white wine
36-40 mussels, scrubbed
  clean and beards removed
Salt and freshly ground pepper
  to taste

1. Pour oil into a large (3-quart or 1-gallon) enameled stockpot. Add garlic and cook over low heat for 2-3 minutes, taking care that garlic does not brown.

2. Add onions, peppers, tomatoes, parsley, olives, lemon juice, and saffron. Sauté for 5 minutes.

3. Pour in wine and add mussels. Cover the stockpot and steam for 5-10 minutes (depending on the size of the mussels), stirring once or twice while cooking. When the mussels have opened, taste the broth and correct the seasoning. Discard any mussels that have not opened.

4. Ladle 8-10 mussels and 1 cup broth into each of four large shallow bowls and serve. Have an empty soup plate on the table to hold the discarded shells or use the mussel shells to eat the soup from if you like. Serve with toasted French bread to sop up any leftover broth.

# BAHAMAS FISH CHOWDER

Bahamian cooking calls for some unusual combinations. Here, annatto and cinnamon blend to make a slightly sweet bright orange base for the chowder. Annatto, or achiote, is a red seed from the annatto tree, ground to a powder and used for coloring in Caribbean and Indian cooking. It is usually sold in Latin American markets under the name achiote, but may be hard to find in regular supermarkets. If annatto is unavailable, use ground turmeric for color. Likewise, sofrito paste is a pungent blend of spices often used in Caribbean cooking. Look for it in the Hispanic Foods section of the supermarket.

Serves 4

3 tablespoons vegetable oil
3 cloves garlic, peeled and chopped
2 teaspoons sofrito paste
2 jalapeño peppers, seeded and chopped
½ cup chopped white onion
½ cup chopped red bell pepper
½ cup peeled and diced green plantains
½ teaspoon ground cinnamon
1 teaspoon ground turmeric or annatto

1½ pounds fillets of fish such as Nassau grouper, red grouper, pompano, or gray, red, or yellowtail snapper; white-fleshed fish such as turbot may be less costly substitutes
5 cups fish stock (see Index)
2 dashes hot pepper sauce
Salt to taste
Chopped scallion greens or a sprinkling of ground turmeric for garnish

1. Heat oil in a 3-quart Dutch oven over medium heat. Add garlic, sofrito paste, jalapeños, onions, red peppers, and plantains. Sauté until soft, about 15 minutes. Stir often.

2. Add cinnamon, 1 teaspoon turmeric or annato, and fish. Cover with fish stock and simmer gently, uncovered, for 10-15 minutes, until fish flakes with a fork.

3. Separate fillets into bite-sized pieces. Add pepper sauce and salt. Serve hot with a garnish of scallions or turmeric.

# FOUR-LETTUCE SOUP

*An easy-to-make soup, starring the first garden greens of spring. Float a tangle of feathery, shredded lettuce (I use a combination of four varieties) in each bowl of lemony broth—this is a great soup for a light lunch.*

Serves 4

3 cups loosely packed, shredded lettuce leaves such as a combination of baby Bibb, red leaf, butterhead, oak leaf, escarole, and romaine; avoid iceberg
3 cups Golden Garlic Broth or chicken stock (see Index)

½ cup cored and minced green apple
1 tablespoon fresh lemon juice
1 teaspoon sugar
Salt to taste
1-2 tablespoons toasted sliced almonds or paper-thin green apple slices for garnish

1. Wash lettuce leaves. Leave small leaves whole and shred mature lettuce into bite-sized pieces. Drain well and let stand.

2. In a 2-quart nonreactive saucepan, blend broth, apples, lemon juice, and sugar over low heat. Bring to a simmer and cook until apple bits are tender, about 10 minutes. Taste broth and add salt if necessary.

3. Stir lettuce leaves into broth and serve immediately, garnished with a sprinkling of toasted almonds or two or three thin slices of green apple for each bowl.

# SUGAR SNAP PEA SOUP

*Late spring brings the first harvest of sugar snap peas. Although
you may be tempted to eat them raw out of hand, the young,
tender pods make a delicious soup. If the pods are tough and
fibrous, substitute frozen shelled peas.*

Serves 6

3 tablespoons vegetable oil
1½ pounds sugar snap peas,
   washed, trimmed, and
   chopped
2 tablespoons chopped fresh
   chervil or mint *or* 1
   teaspoon dried
1 cup water
1 quart chicken or vegetable
   stock (see Index)

2 tablespoons potato starch
   (see Note)
2 tablespoons water
¼ cup light cream or plain
   nonfat yogurt
Salt and freshly ground pepper
   to taste

1 Pour oil into a large Dutch oven and place over medium heat.
  Add sugar snap peas and chervil or mint. Sauté for 3 minutes,
  stirring often. Add water and bring to a simmer. Turn heat to
  low, cover, and steam until pods are tender, about 12-15
  minutes.

2 Remove pot from heat and let cool for 5-10 minutes. Use a
  slotted spoon to transfer peas to a food processor fitted with
  the steel blade and process until smooth.

3 Place pea puree back in pot, add stock, and turn heat to
  medium-low. Bring puree to a simmer and reduce heat to
  keep it from boiling.

4 In a cup, mix potato starch with water until smooth (add more water if lumpy). Add ½ cup of the hot pea soup and blend. Return the thickened pea mixture to the rest of the soup in the pot and whisk until soup thickens slightly.

5 Add cream, salt, and pepper to taste and serve immediately.

*Note: Potato starch is available in the kosher food section of most supermarkets.*

# CREAM OF NEW POTATO

❧ ❧

*When new potatoes arrive, tiny as walnuts, buy a few pounds of both red and white varieties to make this delicious soup. There is no need to peel the potatoes—tender shreds of skin give extra texture to the soup.*

Serves 4-6

> 1 ½-pound ham hock
> 1½ quarts water
> 1 pound white new potatoes,
>   scrubbed
> 1 pound red new potatoes,
>   scrubbed
> 1 cup sour cream
> Salt and freshly ground pepper
>   to taste
> Paprika and chopped fresh
>   parsley for garnish

1. Simmer ham hock in the water in a 3-quart saucepan for 2 hours. Remove and discard ham hock. Strain stock, chill, and remove fat.

2. Bring defatted stock to a simmer. Cut potatoes in half. Add to saucepan and cook until fork tender—about 10-15 minutes.

3. Using a slotted spoon, transfer 2 cups cooked potatoes from the pot to a blender or a food processor fitted with the steel blade. Add sour cream and process until pureed.

4. Return the potato puree to the saucepan and stir. Season with salt and pepper, garnish with paprika and chopped parsley, and serve hot.

# PUREE OF SPINACH

❧ ❦

*Although it sounds improbable, it's possible to make a thick, creamy soup without adding a lot of fat. This recipe uses a whopping 3 pounds of spinach, pureed with plain nonfat yogurt and powdered nonfat dry milk to achieve the consistency of cream.*

Serves 4

3 pounds fresh spinach, washed and all stems removed, to yield approximately 1½ pound leaves
3 tablespoons water
2 cups plain nonfat yogurt
½ cup skim milk
¾ cup Golden Garlic Broth (see Index)

¼ cup nonfat dry milk
2 cloves garlic, peeled and chopped
1 tablespoon grated lemon zest
4 tablespoons minced red bell pepper for garnish

1. Chop spinach and pack into a 3-quart saucepan that has a tight-fitting lid. Add water. Steam over medium heat for 5 minutes or until spinach is wilted but still bright green.

2. Mix all remaining ingredients in a blender on high speed. Add two-thirds of the cooked spinach and puree again. Return puree to saucepan and stir.

3. Heat over low heat until warmed through. Garnish with a tablespoon of red pepper and serve hot.

# LAMB AND BARLEY SOUP

*This is a flavorful, hearty soup—perfect main-course fare on those chilly early spring days.*

Serves 6

4 pounds lamb shanks or ribs, trimmed of all visible fat
2 quarts water
1 medium-sized white onion, quartered
4 medium-sized carrots, scrubbed and trimmed
¾ cup barley
1 bay leaf
2 cups well-washed and chopped leek
2 cups fresh or frozen, thawed shelled peas

3 tablespoons tomato paste
Juice of one-half lemon
2-3 tablespoons red wine vinegar
2 tablespoons chopped fresh parsley
1 tablespoon chopped fresh thyme
Salt and freshly ground pepper to taste

1 Place lamb, water, onion, and carrots in a large stockpot over high heat. Bring to a boil and skim off foam. Reduce heat and simmer for 2 hours or until meat is falling off bones. Water should be reduced by one-third.

2 Remove from heat and strain, reserving meat. Cool stock and refrigerate. While stock chills, remove meat from cooled bones. Chop meat into small pieces.

3 When stock has chilled, remove any congealed fat from surface with a slotted spoon. Measure defatted stock; there should be 1½ quarts. If less, add water to equal 1½ quarts. Place stock in the pot and bring to a simmer over medium heat. Add barley and bay leaf; cook, covered, over medium heat for 45 minutes.

4 Skim soup and add all remaining ingredients, including reserved chopped meat. Simmer uncovered for 15 minutes and adjust seasonings. Remove bay leaf and serve hot with bread (try a good-quality rye or pumpernickel).

# TROUT AND GARDEN VEGETABLE SOUP

*If you are lucky enough to catch trout when they are in season in early June, be sure to save the trimmings and leftover fillet scraps for this soup. If trout is unavailable, you may use other white-fleshed fish instead.*

Serves 4-6

Heads, tails, and bones of 4-5 trout rinsed (about 3 pounds)
1 cup chopped white onion
¼ cup chopped fresh parsley
1 teaspoon dried thyme *or* 1 tablespoon fresh thyme leaves
1 bay leaf
1 teaspoon freshly ground white pepper
5 cups water

1 cup dry white wine
½ cup thinly sliced carrot
½ cup thinly sliced celery
½ cup shelled fresh or frozen, thawed peas
½ cup well-washed and thinly sliced leek
½ cup sliced fresh mushrooms
1 tablespoon chopped fresh dill
1 cup chopped trout fillets

1. Place trout trimmings, onion, parsley, thyme, bay leaf, and pepper in a 3-quart nonreactive saucepan. Pour in water and turn heat to medium. Bring to a boil and skim. Simmer, uncovered, for 1 hour. Remove from heat and strain.

2. Return strained broth to the saucepan. Add all remaining ingredients except chopped trout fillets, cover and simmer for 20 minutes.

3. Add chopped trout and simmer for 5 minutes more or until trout flakes. Serve immediately.

# CREAM OF PARSLEY

*Parsley has been called "the jewel of herbs," probably because it bedecks so many dishes with its gorgeous greenery. Here, tender spring parsley is made the flavorful star of a cream soup, which is delicious hot or cold. For a lower-fat version, use 2 cups skim milk with ⅓ cup nonfat dry milk stirred in rather than the rich half-and-half.*

Serves 4-6

2 tablespoons unsalted butter
2 tablespoons all-purpose flour
2 cups half-and-half
¼ cup minced red onion
2 cups finely chopped fresh
  parsley
1½ cups beef stock or Very
  Brown Veal Stock (see Index)

½ teaspoon grated lemon zest
1 teaspoon salt
½ teaspoon hot red pepper
  flakes
6 very thin lemon slices for
  garnish

1 Melt butter in a 2-quart saucepan over medium-low heat. Stir in flour to make a roux and cook until smooth, golden, and pasty. Slowly whisk in half-and-half, a few tablespoons at a time, until smooth. Cook, whisking often, until thickened, about 10 minutes.

2 Stir in onion and parsley and cook uncovered for 10 minutes. Transfer to a blender and puree. Add 1 cup of the stock and puree again. Return mixture to the saucepan and slowly whisk in remaining stock. Mix in lemon zest, salt, and red pepper flakes.

3 Reduce heat to low and simmer, uncovered—but do not boil—for 15-20 minutes or until thickened and creamy. Taste and adjust seasonings. Serve each bowl garnished with a lemon slice.

# ZUCCHINI-PARMESAN SOUP

*The first slender zucchini of late spring are no more than an inch in diameter—use the size to your advantage in this soup.*

Serves 4-6

> 4 cups sliced zucchini in
> ¼-inch rounds
> 1 quart Golden Garlic Broth or
> chicken stock (see Index)
> 1 cup grated Parmesan cheese
> ¼ cup fresh lemon juice
> ¼ cup chopped scallion
> ¼ cup chopped fresh parsley
> 1 teaspoon fennel seeds,
> crushed
> Salt and freshly ground white
> pepper to taste
> Grated Parmesan cheese and
> Toasted Pita Strips (recipe
> follows) for garnish

1. Place zucchini and broth in a 3-quart saucepan. Bring to a simmer over medium heat and cook uncovered for 5-6 minutes or until zucchini is tender and bright green.

2. Slowly sprinkle Parmesan into soup, stirring constantly. Add lemon juice, scallions, parsley, and seasonings. Cook until cheese melts.

3. Taste and adjust seasonings. Serve with Toasted Pita Strips and extra Parmesan if desired.

# TOASTED PITA STRIPS

1 pita bread
3 tablespoons olive oil

Preheat oven to 400°F. Separate pita in half to form two rounds. Cut into narrow strips and toss with oil. Spread on a nonstick cookie sheet and toast for 8-10 minutes or until crispy and browned. Let cool and sprinkle on top of soup as garnish.

# GUMBO

*On my last trip to New Orleans I shipped my clothes home so I could carry fresh crawfish and andouille sausage back to Chicago to make gumbo. This is a surprisingly fast recipe to make, and it freezes quite well.*

Serves 8

¼ cup chicken fat (see Note)
¼ cup all-purpose flour
½ cup minced celery
½ cup minced Spanish onion
½ cup minced red bell pepper
½ cup minced green bell pepper
1 tablespoon minced garlic
3 sprigs fresh thyme
1 bay leaf
2 pounds andouille sausage, casing removed and meat chopped

1 pound crawfish meat, cleaned and rinsed
1 pound boneless, skinless chicken thighs
½ pound crab claws, cracked and rinsed
2½ cups water
2½ cups fresh or frozen okra
1 teaspoon cayenne pepper
Hot pepper sauce (as much as you can stand)
1 cup cooked long-grain white rice as an accompaniment

1. Place chicken fat in a heavy 3-quart stockpot and melt over medium heat. Add flour to make a roux and cook until the mixture turns brown, stirring constantly. The flour should be completely emulsified in the fat, and the roux should be very smooth.

2. Reduce the heat and add celery, onion, bell peppers, garlic, and herbs, stirring well to coat the vegetables with the roux. Sauté for 15 minutes. While vegetables cook, brown the sausage in a 9-inch skillet. Lift browned sausage out of skillet, reserving fat in pan. Add sausage, crawfish, chicken, crab, and water to vegetable mixture in stockpot. Reduce heat and simmer.

3. Sauté okra in sausage drippings over medium heat until bubbly (about 10 minutes) and scrape into stockpot. Add cayenne and pepper sauce to taste, stir well, and simmer until thickened, about 20 minutes. Taste and adjust seasonings.

4. To serve, place a spoonful of rice in the bottom of a large soup plate. Pour gumbo over it, making sure each serving has plenty of sausage, chicken, and shellfish. The gumbo will keep in the refrigerator for up to 2 days.

*Note: Chicken fat may be trimmed from the thighs called for here, or purchased, prepackaged, at the meat or deli counter of most supermarkets.*

# ASPARAGUS CREME

*A thick bright green soup—prepared without heavy cream— best made when asparagus is plentiful and cheap.*

Serves 4

> 3 pounds asparagus, woody
>    ends trimmed off
> 1 quart chicken stock (see
>    Index)
> 1 large egg white
> 1 cup plain nonfat yogurt
> 1 teaspoon salt
> ½ teaspoon freshly ground
>    white pepper
> ½ teaspoon grated lemon zest
> 1 teaspoon minced fresh
>    parsley
> Toasted pine nuts for garnish

1. Cut off asparagus tips 1 inch from top and reserve. Chop remaining stems. Place stems in a 2-quart soup pot with stock and bring to a simmer over medium heat.

2. When asparagus is just tender (about 10 minutes) turn off heat. Lift asparagus stems out of stock and place in a blender along with 2 cups of the stock. Blend on high speed until smooth. Strain through a sieve back into the soup pot.

3. Blend egg white into yogurt along with salt, pepper, lemon zest, and parsley. Add the yogurt mixture to the asparagus puree and whisk well. Cook for 5 minutes over medium-low heat, stirring often.

4. Stir in reserved asparagus tips and cook until tips are bright green and tender, about 10 minutes. Ladle into serving bowls and garnish with pine nuts.

# SPRING VEGETABLE SOUP

*Dieters will love this light soup developed by Alex Panozzo of the Heartland Spa, as it has just 50 calories per 8-ounce serving. If you prefer a richer soup, use beef stock instead of vegetable stock.*

Serves 6

Vegetable oil cooking spray
1 cup well-washed and sliced leeks (cut in half lengthwise, then into ½-inch slices)
½ cup thinly sliced celery
½ cup thinly sliced carrot
⅓ cup thinly sliced turnip
⅓ cup ½-inch-thick yellow squash slices
1 teaspoon fennel seeds, crushed
½ teaspoon dried rosemary
½ teaspoon dried thyme
4¼ cups vegetable stock (see Index)
½ cup frozen peas, thawed
1 tablespoon chopped fresh parsley
⅛ teaspoon salt
Freshly ground pepper to taste
1½ cups very thinly sliced spinach or Swiss chard leaves

1. Spray a 12-inch nonstick skillet evenly with vegetable oil cooking spray. Set skillet over medium heat and add leeks, celery, carrots, turnips, and squash. Sauté, stirring often, until vegetables are fork-tender, about 15–20 minutes. Add fennel, rosemary, and thyme; stir and sauté for 1 minute longer. Remove from heat.

2. Put sautéed vegetables in a 3-quart soup pot over medium heat. Pour in stock and bring to a simmer. Partially cover pot, reduce heat to low, and cook for 10 minutes. Add peas, parsley, salt, and pepper. Simmer for 3 minutes more. Taste and adjust seasonings if necessary.

3. Place ¼ cup of the spinach or chard in the bottom of each soup bowl. Ladle 1 cup of soup over the greens and serve immediately.

# STRAWBERRY SOUP

*When June sunshine arrives, strawberries ripen to an intensely flavored, juicy sweetness. For this velvety fruit soup I use a Johannesburg Riesling from Fetzer Vineyards—it blends superbly with the fresh berries.*

*Woodruff is a perennial herb, native to northern Europe, with a slightly sweet aroma and a piquant taste. It is sold fresh and in dried form at specialty supermarkets and by mail order (see Appendix). If you don't have woodruff on hand, you may substitute a teaspoon of minced orange zest instead.*

Serves 4

5 sprigs woodruff *or* 1 teaspoon minced orange zest

2 teaspoons sugar

1 cup good-quality Riesling wine

3 cups strawberries, hulled and sliced, with juices

2 cups nonfat vanilla yogurt

2 tablespoons strawberry spreadable fruit (no sugar added)

4 strawberries, each cut into quarters, for garnish

1. Crush woodruff sprigs, or orange zest, with sugar in a 2-quart glass bowl. Add wine and mix well. Cover and let steep for several hours.

2. Pour wine mixture through a fine-mesh strainer into a small bowl and discard residue. Combine strained wine mixture and strawberries in a large bowl and chill for several hours.

3. Mix yogurt with spreadable fruit in a 2-quart tureen or serving bowl. Using a slotted spoon, transfer the strawberries from the wine mixture to the tureen. Add wine mixture to taste. (I use all of the wine, but others may prefer a less pronounced wine taste.) Cover and chill for 1-2 hours. Serve cold, garnished with fresh strawberry quarters arranged in petal formation.

# 3
# SUMMER

Cold soups are the mainstay of my summer kitchen. When the heat is intense and even a half hour of cooking time next to a stove seems unbearable, I rely on fast soups made with vegetables and cold stock, yogurt, or cream. Such soups are almost effortless to make, truly "no sweat."

Several recipes, such as Cream of Red Peppers with Walnuts, may be served hot or cold. Others are strictly cold soups, such as the Cold Mango Cantaloupe Soup.

Clams and oysters from both coasts are in season starting in June. Several varieties of melon—honeydew, casaba, and cantaloupe—make excellent salads to accompany a light meal of soup. Peppers, squashes, and cucumbers are plentiful and inexpensive, particularly late in summer. Take advantage of the low prices for red and yellow bell peppers by buying a few pounds to roast and freeze.

Because outdoor gatherings are casual and food choices greater than at any other time of year, entertaining seems easier in summer. Make the most of the combination of warm weather and fresh-from-the-farmer's-market produce with the recipes that follow.

# COLD MANGO CANTALOUPE SOUP

*Mangoes have a distinctive mellow flavor but can be tricky to cut due to the seed in the center. The easiest way to cube a mango is to slice it in half, cutting close to the wide, flat pit. Cut away the pit. Hold one half cut side up. Score the flesh inside the skin with diagonal slices, leaving the skin intact. Be sure to cut to, not through, the skin. Score again in the opposite direction, creating a grid of slices.*

*Hold the mango over a bowl and press the center of the skin to turn the mango inside out. The cubes of fruit will stand away from the skin like the quills of a porcupine. Slice them off the skin into the bowl and squeeze the skin to obtain the juices.*

Serves 4-6

3 mangoes, peeled, seeded, and chopped (see instructions above; about 3-4 cups fruit, including juice)
2 cups peeled, seeded, and chopped cantaloupe
½ cup sugar
2 cups dry white wine
2 cups water
2 tablespoons orange juice concentrate
½ teaspoon ground ginger
¼ teaspoon freshly grated nutmeg
Salt and freshly ground pepper to taste
Thin slices of cantaloupe or finely chopped candied ginger for garnish

1. Place all the ingredients except garnish in a 3-quart nonreactive saucepan over medium heat. Bring to a simmer and skim off any foam.

2. Reduce heat to low and simmer for 15 minutes or until fruit is pulpy and soft. Press half the soup through a food mill or puree in a blender. Return puree to saucepan and stir well. Taste and adjust seasonings.

3. Remove soup from heat and chill thoroughly. Garnish with slivers of cantaloupe or finely chopped candied ginger and serve.

# BLUEBERRY SOUP

*The Canyon Ranch Spa in the Berkshires serves small portions of this refreshing fruit soup at midday. With only 75 calories per ¾ cup serving, it makes a great low-cal snack or breakfast soup.*

Serves 4

> ⅓ cup frozen unsweetened
>   pineapple juice concentrate
> ½ cup water
> 1 teaspoon fresh lemon juice
> 3 cups fresh blueberries,
>   washed

1. Combine the juice concentrate, water, and lemon juice in a blender. Add 2 cups of the blueberries and blend until smooth.

2. Combine puree with remaining blueberries and mix well. Chill and serve cold.

# ZUPPA DI ZUKE

*A lighthearted approach to soup making holds sway in the kitchen of Patti and Jerry Bock in Pound Ridge, New York. "My feeling," says Patti, "is that soup is one of the most satisfying foods on earth. I think everyone would love to be able to spend hours making soup, but because most of us don't have time, this soup is my favorite."*

Serves 4

| | |
|---|---|
| 2 tablespoons unsalted butter or olive oil | 1 teaspoon curry powder |
| | 1 teaspoon salt |
| 2 pounds zucchini, sliced into paper-thin rounds | Freshly ground pepper to taste |
| | Half-and-half for garnish |
| 2 cups chilled chicken or vegetable stock (see Index) | (approximately 1-1½ cups) |

1. Put the butter in a large sauté pan that has a tight-fitting lid. Melt over medium-low heat. Add zucchini, stir, and cover. A few minutes later, shake the pan and stir again.

2. In 10 minutes, test the zucchini with a fork; it should be pearly green, translucent, and soft.

3. Put half the zucchini into a blender along with 1 cup of the broth, curry, salt, and pepper and blend on the "chop" setting. Do not overblend; the mixture should still be a little coarse. Pour into a serving bowl. Repeat with remaining zucchini and broth and mix with soup in serving bowl. The soup should have the texture of a split pea soup.

4. Taste and adjust seasonings. Ladle into chilled bowls and pass a small pitcher of cold half-and-half, to be swirled into each serving with a spoon.

# WATERCRESS AND POTATO SOUP

*No need to pepper this cold soup: the pungent watercress will supply all the heat you'd want on a steamy summer day.*

Serves 4-6

2 cups water
1 teaspoon salt
1 whole chicken breast (about 1 pound)
2 cups peeled and diced white potato in ½-inch cubes
2 cups sour cream or plain nonfat yogurt

1 cup chopped watercress leaves
Freshly ground white pepper to taste (optional)
Watercress sprigs for garnish

1. Bring water and salt to a boil in a 2-quart saucepan. Skin and poach chicken breast in water for 10-15 minutes or until well done.

2. Remove chicken from water. Add potatoes and cook until tender, about 20-25 minutes. Reduce heat to a simmer. Chop cooked chicken breast meat (1 whole breast will yield just over 1 cup chopped meat) and discard bones.

3. Stir ⅓ cup of the hot cooking water into sour cream or yogurt. When warmed, return to the pot along with the chopped chicken and watercress. Stir well and cook for 5 minutes more or until heated through.

4. Taste and adjust seasonings; add a dash of white pepper if desired. Refrigerate soup for several hours. Garnish each bowl with a sprig of watercress before serving.

# CHILLED PAPAYA SOUP

*Papayas are an excellent source of vitamin C, especially when served raw. The following recipe, from the New Orleans–based food writer John DeMers, was originally published in* Caribbean Cooking.

Serves 6

> 3 medium-sized papayas
> (about 2½–3 pounds total)
> 1½ cups water
> ⅓ cup fresh lime juice, or to
> taste
> ½ cup brandy
> Paper-thin lime slices for
> garnish

1 Peel the papayas, scoop out seeds, and cut one of the fruits into 24 cubes. Reserve.

2 Place remaining papaya in a blender and add water; puree on high speed until smooth. Pour into a bowl and add lime juice in small amounts, tasting until it reaches the desired tartness.

3 Whisk in brandy, cover, and refrigerate until well chilled, about 2 hours. To serve, place four of the reserved papaya cubes in each bowl, pour soup on top, and serve. Garnish with a lime slice.

# BEEFY BEET BORSCHT

*Borscht, the hearty beet soup that is a traditional dish among Eastern Europeans, is good hot or cold. I often make this soup in the early morning, before the sun's heat conspires with my stove to make cooking unbearable. The soup then has all day to chill in the refrigerator and allow the flavors to meld.*

Serves 6

3 tablespoons vegetable oil
1 pound boneless beef stew
  meat
2 quarts water
3 cups sliced beets in ½-inch
  julienne strips
3 cups sliced carrot in ½-inch
  julienne strips
2 cups diced red potato

1 cup chopped red onion
1 cup chopped dill pickle
3 tablespoons tomato paste
2 tablespoons fresh chopped
  dill
2 tablespoons minced garlic
1 teaspoon salt
Hot red pepper flakes to taste

[1] Place oil in a large soup pot over high heat. Sear beef meat until well browned in hot oil, stirring to brown evenly. Reduce heat and add water. Simmer, partially covered, for 45 minutes, skimming off foam as needed.

[2] Add all vegetables to the soup pot along with pickles, tomato paste, dill, garlic, salt, and red pepper flakes. Let cook for 20-30 minutes or until vegetables are crisp-tender. Remove from heat. Taste and adjust seasonings.

[3] If desired, chill and remove fat from soup before serving. This not only cuts calories but improves the flavor as well. Serve hot or cold, with plenty of fresh, crusty bread.

# TOMATO ROSEMARY SOUP

*The keys to the success of this recipe are vine-ripened tomatoes and plenty of fresh rosemary. Although a passable version of this soup may be made with canned tomato puree and dried rosemary it cannot match the intense flavor or chunky texture of the fresh version. It may be served cold or hot.*

Serves 8

½ cup chopped sweet or mild
  onion
¼ cup olive oil
¼ cup all-purpose flour
1½ cups skim or whole milk
8 cups seeded and chopped
  fresh or canned tomatoes

⅓ cup packed chopped fresh
  rosemary *or* 3 tablespoons
  dried rosemary, crushed
  with a little vegetable oil
Salt and freshly ground pepper
  to taste

1. In a 9-inch skillet, sauté onions in oil over low heat until soft. Using a slotted spoon to keep onions in the skillet, strain the onion-flavored oil into a 3-quart nonreactive Dutch oven. Remove skillet from heat, reserving onions.

2. Whisk flour with oil in pot and cook over medium-low heat to make a roux that is smooth and golden brown. Slowly whisk in milk, a few tablespoons at a time, and cook until thickened. Stir often to prevent sticking or lumping. Taste to make sure the raw flour flavor has disappeared. Add onions and any accumulated cooking juices in the skillet to the Dutch oven and stir well.

3. Add 2 cups of the tomatoes to the milk mixture and blend well, whisking until smooth. Add rosemary and bring to a simmer.

4. Mix in remaining tomatoes, beating well to mash the tomato into bits as it cooks, and heat through. Taste and season with salt and pepper. Serve hot or let cool and then refrigerate until chilled and serve cold.

56

# ICED SUMMER SQUASH CREAM

*Even in the heat of August, you can enjoy this soup without heating up your kitchen. That's because the squash is cooked in the microwave.*

Serves 4

4 cups seeded and finely chopped yellow squash
1 tablespoon water
2 tablespoons cream
10 ounces tofu, extra soft, drained and crumbled
3 ice cubes
1 teaspoon sugar
½ teaspoon salt
¼ teaspoon freshly grated nutmeg

½ teaspoon garam masala (Indian spice mixture sold at specialty food stores)
¼ teaspoon freshly ground white pepper
¼ cup plain nonfat yogurt mixed with 1 tablespoon mild curry powder for garnish

1. Place prepared squash in a microwave-safe container, sprinkle with water, cover tightly, and microwave on high for 6 minutes or until tender and bright yellow.

2. Let squash cool. Place in a blender along with cream, tofu, ice cubes, and seasonings. Blend on high speed until smooth and creamy.

3. Refrigerate for 2 hours. Taste and adjust seasonings. Serve in chilled glass bowls with a dollop of curried yogurt.

# BASIL TOMATO POTATO SOUP

*The sweet, spicy taste of basil enlivens the bland base of boiled potatoes, while the chunks of tomato add texture and color.*

Serves 4-6

4 cups peeled and cubed white
   boiling (California whites)
   potato
1 quart water
1 cup chopped fresh basil
   leaves
4 cups seeded and finely
   chopped very ripe tomato

2 tablespoons cider vinegar
2 teaspoons celery salt
1 teaspoon freshly ground
   white pepper
Sour cream or plain nonfat
   yogurt and paprika for
   garnish

1. Bring potatoes and water to boil in a 3-quart saucepan. Cook until potatoes are very tender, about 30 minutes. Remove half the potatoes from the boiling water with a slotted spoon and puree, with a cup of the cooking water, in a blender on high speed. Add the basil and puree again.

2. Return the puree to the pot and stir in the tomatoes. Add vinegar, celery salt, and white pepper. Taste and adjust seasonings.

3. Garnish with a dollop of sour cream or yogurt and a sprinkling of paprika and serve hot or let cool, refrigerate until chilled, garnish, and serve cold.

*Note: I like the texture of bits of tomato skin, but if you don't care for it, peel the tomatoes by pouring boiling water over them in a bowl, just enough to cover. Let sit for 3 minutes, or until skins start to split. Drain, continue removing skins under cold running water, then seed and chop.*

# CORN AND OYSTER CHOWDER

*Fresh sweet corn and briny oysters combine to make this creamy chowder a distinctive dish, perfect for entertaining a crowd. Based on a recipe from my grandmother, this elegant chowder is deceptively simple to make.*

Serves 8-10

2 cups water
8 ears sweet corn, shucked and cobs scraped to yield 4 cups fresh corn kernels and juices
2 cups half-and-half
½ teaspoon freshly ground pepper

1¼ quarts (approximately 30) shucked fresh oysters with their liquor
1 teaspoon salt
Hot pepper sauce to taste
Oyster crackers or chopped watercress for garnish

1. Place water in a 1-gallon stockpot and add corn, half-and-half, and pepper; heat over medium heat until simmering. Cook for 10 minutes.

2. Drain oyster liquor into stockpot and bring back to a simmer. Rinse oysters.

3. Add oysters and salt to stockpot, reduce heat, and heat through, about 3-5 minutes (depending on size of oysters). Add hot pepper sauce to taste. Serve hot with a sprinkling of crushed crackers or chopped watercress.

# CREAM OF RED PEPPERS WITH WALNUTS

*Based on an old Armenian recipe for a dip, this soup blends the mellow smokiness of roasted red peppers with the somewhat bitter taste of walnuts. It may be served hot or cold.*

*Be sure to toast the walnuts until just golden and discard any that burn, as they will be too bitter. In a pinch, use bottled roasted red peppers and add a little more paprika for flavor.*

Serves 4-6

3 tablespoons olive oil
¾ cup shelled walnuts
3 cups roasted and chopped
  red bell pepper (see Note)
1 cup chopped white onion
3 cloves garlic, crushed
2 teaspoons paprika

1 tablespoon cayenne pepper
1 teaspoon salt
1 teaspoon ground cumin
1¼ cups half-and-half
1¼ cups beef stock (see Index)
Freshly ground pepper to taste
Pomegranate seeds for garnish

1 Place oil in a heavy 9-inch skillet. Sauté walnuts over medium heat until golden brown. Stir in roasted red pepper, onion, and garlic. Sauté for 5 minutes, stirring often. Remove skillet from the heat and scrape pepper-nut mixture into a food processor fitted with the steel blade.

2 Process peppers and nuts until smooth. Add seasonings and half-and-half. Process again until creamy.

3 Pour beef stock into a 3-quart saucepan and bring to a simmer over medium heat. Gradually whisk in the puree. Reduce heat and cook until heated through. Taste and adjust seasonings. Serve warm or cold, garnished with a tablespoon or two of pomegranate seeds, with plenty of warm pita bread.

*Note: To make your own roasted red peppers, take advantage of the searing heat of a barbecue grill. While waiting for the coals to turn gray for your barbecue, place whole red peppers on the grill. Blacken the peppers completely, turning them with tongs. The pepper skin will blister and peel. When the peppers are completely black on the outside, remove from the grill. If you like, place peppers in paper bag to "sweat" and let them cool enough to be handled; then remove shreds of skin. Use a paring knife to remove any stubborn bits of skin. Cut the softened red flesh away from the seeded core and chop for this recipe. You can also roast red peppers over the flame of a gas stove burner or under an electric broiler—be sure to use tongs with an insulated handle to hold the peppers above the heat source. Roasted peppers freeze well, so consider buying lots of peppers when their price is low.*

# PEPPER AND CORN TORTILLA SOUP

*Fragrant red peppers, strips of jalapeño, and crispy tortilla noodles make this soup a feast for the senses. Traditional recipes call for lots of cumin and oregano, but I prefer the pepper flavor instead.*

Serves 6

5 tablespoons corn oil
2 cups chopped red bell
  pepper
3 medium jalapeño peppers,
  seeded and sliced very thin
3 cloves garlic, peeled and
  minced

5 cups strong chicken stock
  (see Index)
Juice of one small lime
6 6-inch corn tortillas
⅓ cup chopped cilantro leaves,
  avocado slices, and chopped
  ripe tomato for garnish

1. Preheat oven to 400°F. Heat 2 tablespoons of the corn oil in a 2-quart Dutch oven. Add red peppers, jalapeños, and garlic and sauté over low heat for 20 minutes. Pour in chicken stock and lime juice and simmer, about 10 minutes.

2. While vegetables cook, stack tortillas on top of each other. Cut the whole stack in half and then cut each half, width-wise, into strips no more than ½ inch wide.

3. Brush a cookie sheet with remaining 3 tablespoons corn oil and place tortilla strips on it, tossing to coat the strips lightly. Toast in oven for 10-15 minutes until brown, stirring occasionally to prevent burning.

4. To serve, place toasted tortilla strips in bowl and pour 1 cup of hot soup over them. Garnish with a sprinkling of cilantro, some avocado slices, and chopped ripe tomato.

# GREENS SOUP

*An exceptionally easy, quick soup made from dark leafy greens. Beet, collard, mustard, turnip greens, and Swiss chard fare best when cooked in a rich stock that balances their pungency. Don't avoid dark greens just because they are more bitter than spinach or cabbage. Instead, choose greens with small leaves and trim off fibrous stems. If only the mature, large-leafed greens are available, remove stems and tear the greens off the stringy center of each leaf. Chop or tear the leaves into smaller bits that will cook quickly. Simmer greens just until tender, no more than 10–15 minutes, to preserve nutrients.*

Serves 4-6

2 quarts strong Very Brown Beef Stock or Spicy Pork Stock (see Index)
¾ cup white long-grain rice
5 cups chopped greens
1 pound cooked smoked sausage such as kielbasa, diced

1 28-ounce can tomato puree
1 teaspoon dried sage
½ teaspoon hot red pepper flakes
1 teaspoon garlic salt
Hot red pepper flakes or lemon slices for garnish

1. Place beef stock in a large soup pot over medium heat and bring to a simmer. Add rice and cover. Cook for 5 minutes.

2. Add greens, sausage, tomato puree, and seasonings. Cook for 10-15 minutes, depending on degree of tenderness desired for greens. Taste soup and adjust seasonings. Serve hot with a sprinkling of red pepper flakes or a slice of lemon.

# CREAMY LEEK SOUP

*The slightly chewy texture of sautéed leeks blends well with the creaminess of pureed potatoes. This is a good soup to make ahead and chill. If you do, be sure not to add the final fillip of crème fraîche or sour cream until serving time.*

*Make cleaning the leeks easier by grasping one at the root end and slicing lengthwise toward the greens, keeping the knobby base intact. The leek will fan out in a sink full of water, allowing you to get the grit out from all the layers. I recommend two or three washings to remove all the dirt.*

Serves 4-6

2 quarts chicken or turkey stock (see Index)
4 cups well-washed and thinly sliced leek
2 cups peeled and finely shredded white boiling potato
Salt and freshly ground white pepper to taste

½ cup crème fraîche or sour cream (see Note)
Chopped fresh parsley and crisp-cooked bacon, crumbled, for garnish (optional)

1. Place stock in a large soup pot over medium heat and bring to a simmer. Add leeks and potatoes and simmer for 15 minutes or until leek greens are tender.

2. Reduce heat, taste, and adjust seasonings. If you wish to serve cold, let the soup cool, then chill it. In a measuring cup, mix a small amount of hot stock with the crème fraîche and return mixture to soup pot, stirring well. Ladle soup into large soup bowls and garnish with parsley and bacon bits if desired.

*Note:* Low-fat sour cream or yogurt that is not gelatin-based may be substituted for the crème fraîche. Gelatin-based light or nonfat "sour cream" or yogurt will curdle into unappetizing lumps rather than melting into the soup base. Read the ingredients list on any light dairy product, including nonfat plain yogurt, before adding it to a hot stock.

# CONFETTI CHOWDER WITH SALMON

*Bright green, red, and yellow vegetables and pink salmon against the white creamy broth make this chowder look as if confetti has been tossed into the pot.*

Serves 4-6

1 tablespoon olive oil
1 cup diced red bell pepper
1 pound fresh salmon steak, skinned and boned
2 cups fish stock (see Index)
2 cups fresh corn, scraped off cobs *or* 1 16-ounce can corn, packed without sugar
2 tablespoons chopped fresh parsley

½ teaspoon freshly ground white pepper
1 teaspoon snipped fresh chives
1 cup half-and-half
1 teaspoon Hungarian hot paprika
Salt and freshly ground pepper to taste

1. Place olive oil in a 4-quart soup pot and set over medium heat. Add the red bell pepper and stir often until fork-tender.

2. Lay salmon steaks on top of peppers in the pot and cover. Steam for 4-5 minutes.

3. Pour in stock, corn and its juices, parsley, white pepper, and chives. Blend with a fork to break up salmon into bite-sized pieces.

4. Reduce heat to low, stir in half-and-half and let warm through, about 5 minutes. Add paprika, salt, and pepper to taste and serve hot.

# LEMON CUCUMBER SOUP

*Look for firm, unblemished and unwaxed pickling cucumbers for this virtuously low-cal, broth-based soup. For the best flavor, use only freshly squeezed lemon juice.*

Serves 4

> 1 quart Golden Garlic Broth
> (see Index)
> ½ cup long-grain white rice
> 2 cups washed, seeded, and
> diced pickling cucumbers
> ¼ cup fresh lemon juice
> Salt and freshly ground pepper
> to taste
> ¼ cup minced scallion greens

1. Bring broth to a simmer in a 2-quart saucepan. Add rice and cook, covered, for 15 minutes.

2. Stir in cucumbers and lemon juice. Reduce heat and simmer uncovered for 10 minutes. Add salt and pepper, stir in scallion tops, and serve immediately.

# HOT AND SOUR SOUP

*Make this spicy soup when locally grown red and yellow peppers appear in the market. It's a low-calorie soup from chef Alex Panozzo of the Heartland Spa that can serve as a preface to a salad of Chinese vegetables.*

Serves 8

1½ quarts vegetable stock (see Index)
2 teaspoons rice miso paste
2 teaspoons low-sodium tamari or soy sauce
2 teaspoons rice vinegar
1 teaspoon hot (chili) sesame oil
2 ribs celery, sliced diagonally
1 medium-sized red bell pepper, seeded and slivered
1 medium-sized yellow bell pepper, seeded and slivered

6 reconstituted dried or fresh shiitake mushrooms
1 tablespoon cornstarch or potato starch dissolved in 2 tablespoons cold water
6 scallions, including half of the green tops, sliced diagonally
⅓ cup chopped water chestnuts
Chinese pepper sauce or hot pepper sauce to taste

1 Combine stock, miso, tamari, and vinegar in a 3-quart non-reactive soup pot. Bring to a simmer over medium heat.

2 Heat a 10-inch nonstick skillet to stir-fry vegetables. Add hot sesame oil, followed by celery and peppers. Sauté for 3-5 minutes; then add mushrooms. Fry for 2-3 minutes and add to stock, stirring well.

3 Stir in dissolved starch and stir well, simmering until thickened, about 5 minutes. Add scallions and water chestnuts. Season to taste with pepper sauce and serve immediately.

# MELANGE OF MUSHROOM SOUP

*For the most distinctive flavor, use an assortment of fresh and dried mushrooms in this rich-tasting soup.*

Serves 4

½ cup dark cream sherry
½ cup water
3 pounds fresh mushrooms (a mixture of button, shiitake, chanterelles, porcini, or what's available at the market), cleaned and sliced
3 ounces dried mushrooms (chanterelles, morels, oyster mushrooms, Chinese cloud ears), soaked in warm water to cover to remove grit

5 cups vegetable stock or Golden Garlic Broth (see Index)
1 teaspoon fresh thyme
Salt and freshly ground pepper to taste
½ cup light cream

1. Place sherry and water in a 12-inch nonstick skillet; add fresh mushrooms and sauté for 10 minutes over medium heat. Transfer to a 3-quart soup pot.

2. Add dried mushrooms and stock to the soup pot. Add seasonings and cook until dried mushrooms are tender, about 20 minutes. Remove one half of the mushrooms from soup pot with a slotted spoon. Puree in blender with cream, then return to soup pot.

3. Reduce heat to a simmer. Cover and cook for 15 minutes over medium-low heat or until mushrooms are tender and broth has thickened. Serve hot with Italian bread, focaccia, or crostini.

# FRESH HERB BROTH
# WITH RICOTTA-DILL DUMPLINGS

*The* herbes de Provence *traditionally are used in marinades, salads, and vinaigrettes. I like their summery-fresh flavor in this soup, served with Ricotta-Dill Dumplings.*

Serves 4

1 quart chicken stock (see Index)
¼ cup chopped fresh marjoram
¼ cup chopped fresh thyme
2 tablespoons chopped fresh oregano

2 tablespoons chopped fresh summer savory
Dough for Ricotta-Dill Dumplings (recipe follows)
Salt and freshly ground pepper to taste

1. Put broth and herbs in a 2-quart saucepan set over medium heat. Bring to a simmer and reduce heat to low. Simmer, partially covered, for 20 minutes, making sure the broth does not boil.

2. Make Ricotta-Dill Dumpling dough. Strain broth and return to pot. Bring back to a simmer. Drop dumpling dough from a teaspoon onto the surface of the soup. The dough will puff up slightly.

3. Cook dumplings for 10 minutes. Using a pair of tongs or two spoons, gently turn them over and cook for 5 minutes.

4. Adjust seasonings and serve immediately, with three or four dumplings in each bowl.

# RICOTTA-DILL DUMPLINGS

½ cup part-skim ricotta cheese
1 large egg white
2 cloves garlic, peeled and
    chopped
¾ cup all-purpose flour, plus
    up to ¼ cup if needed
1 teaspoon fresh chopped dill
½ teaspoon salt

1. Place all ingredients in the bowl of a food processor fitted with the steel blade. Process on high until dough forms a ball around the blade (6-7 pulses).

2. If batter is still loose, add more flour and process again. Stop when dough is firm enough to make a ball.

# LOBSTER CATCHERS'
# SEAFOOD CHOWDER

*Restaurant owner Arnie Pinkus shares his recipe for seafood chowder which yields enough chowder for a crowd.*

Serves 8-10

½ cup (¼ pound) unsalted butter
½ cup all-purpose flour
3 tablespoons vegetable oil
2 cups diced carrot
2 cups diced celery
2 cups well-washed and finely chopped leek
½ pound calamari (squid), sliced into ½-inch rings
1 quart milk
3 cups bottled clam juice
1 pound chopped clams in juice
3 tablespoons dry white wine
3 tablespoons *fino* sherry

1 tablespoon Worcestershire sauce
½ teaspoon hot pepper sauce
1 cup cream or half-and-half
1 tablespoon fresh thyme
1 bay leaf
½ teaspoon salt
½ teaspoon freshly ground white pepper
½ teaspoon freshly grated nutmeg
3 tablespoons brandy
1 pound bay scallops, chopped into bite-sized pieces

1. In a heavy 1-quart saucepan, melt butter; then add flour to make a roux, stirring constantly until completely emulsified and roux begins to turn golden. You should smell the aroma of toasted popcorn after 3-5 minutes of cooking, at which point remove roux from heat and set aside to cool.

2. Pour oil into a 2-gallon stockpot, and place over medium heat. Add carrots and sauté for 3 minutes. Add celery and sauté for 3 minutes more; then add leeks. When leeks are tender (about 4-5 minutes), add calamari and sauté for 3 minutes.

3 Pour in milk and bring to a simmer; then whisk in roux, stirring well until roux is completely dissolved in milk. When mixture begins to thicken, pour in clam juice and chopped clams, white wine, sherry, Worcestershire sauce, hot pepper sauce, and cream. Stir until well blended.

4 Add dry seasonings and brandy and stir in; let simmer for 5 minutes. Add scallops and cook for 5 minutes or until scallops are just white and still tender. Serve with chowder crackers.

# 4
# FALL

As the temperature drops, my spirits tend to rise. With summer's humidity gone, a bowl of steaming soup once again regains its appeal. Autumn's first brisk days fill me with energy, making me eager to tackle longer-cooking soups.

Cold snaps also usher in a bounty of fall produce, including apples, broccoli, cabbages, the early winter squashes, potatoes, and late-harvest tomatoes. Bay scallops are in season in the fall, showcased here in Scallop and Potato Chowder. Spicy prepared meats, such as kielbasa sausage, enliven fiber-rich Market Bean Soup. Capture the last taste of vine-ripened tomatoes with Late-Harvest Tomato Soup.

As befits the season, several fall soups call for apples as ingredients, among them Cider and Cheese Soup. I prefer the tangy varieties, such as McIntosh, Northern Spy, and Newtown Pippin or other greenings.

# TURKEY AND MUSHROOM SOUP

*A favorite post-Thanksgiving tradition in my mother's house is boiling the bird's carcass for mushroom soup. Adjust the quantities in this recipe to accommodate different-sized birds.*

Serves 6

1 carcass from a 14-pound
   turkey, with about 2 cups
   leftover meat reserved (see
   Note)
2 cups chopped celery
3 cups chopped carrot
1 large Spanish onion, cut in
   half

1 bay leaf
2 teaspoons dried rubbed sage
1 teaspoon salt
1 teaspoon freshly ground
   pepper
¾ cup pearled barley
3 cups sliced fresh
   mushrooms

1. Place carcass in a 2-gallon stockpot and cover with water (about 1 gallon). Bring to a boil, reduce heat to simmer, and add celery, carrots, onion, and bay leaf. Simmer, uncovered, until water is reduced by one-third, about 45 minutes. Remove carcass, onion, and bay leaf from stock with a large slotted spoon. Let carcass cool and pick off any remaining meat. Chop meat and refrigerate.

2. Add seasonings and barley to stockpot. Simmer for 30 minutes; then add mushrooms and 2-3 cups chopped turkey meat. Simmer for 15-20 minutes more or until barley is soft and fluffy and mushrooms are dark. Add more water if necessary.

3. Taste and adjust seasonings. Serve hot with a tossed salad and cranberry bread.

*Note: A roast turkey yields not only leftovers for casseroles and sandwiches but soup as well. Save leftover slivers of meat to combine with additional scraps that are dislodged after the carcass is boiled.*

# INDIAN CURRY SOUP

*Curries and chutnies have the aroma and golden hue of fall days—lingering warm and sweetly spicy on the palate. Chutney and golden raisins give this soup an appealing, but not overwhelming, note of sweetness.*

Serves 4

¼ cup vegetable oil
1½ pounds skinless and boneless chicken breasts, thighs, or legs
1 cup chopped white onion
4 cloves garlic, peeled and chopped
1 tablespoon curry powder
1 teaspoon ground cumin
1 teaspoon ground turmeric
1 cup peeled and chopped white boiling potatoes in ½-inch cubes

½ cup peeled and sliced carrot in ¼-inch rounds
½ cup golden raisins
½ cup mango chutney
1 quart chicken stock (see Index)
Salt and freshly ground pepper to taste
¼ cup chopped cilantro

1. Pour oil into a 3-quart saucepan and turn heat to medium-high. Add chicken and sear for 5–8 minutes, turning often. Lift browned chicken pieces out of hot oil and set aside.

2. Add onion, garlic, seasonings, potatoes, and carrots to hot oil. Stir often, letting potatoes brown evenly. While potatoes brown about 15 minutes, chop the chicken. When potatoes are browned, add chicken to pot along with raisins, chutney, and chicken stock.

3 Turn down heat and let soup simmer; when chicken is cooked all the way through and raisins have plumped, (about 20 minutes), taste and add more spices and salt or pepper if needed. Stir in cilantro and serve immediately.

*Note: You may make this soup even richer by adding ½ cup grated unsweetened coconut and ¼ cup water at the time of adding the stock. Be warned, however, that even this small amount of coconut adds about 16 grams of fat to each serving.*

# ROASTED EGGPLANT
# AND RED PEPPER PUREE

*This uncomplicated soup takes advantage of the robust flavors
of roasted eggplant and red pepper.*

Serves 4

> 2 medium-sized eggplants
> 1 tablespoon chopped fresh
>    sweet basil
> 2 cloves garlic, crushed
> 1 teaspoon salt
> ½ teaspoon white pepper
> Juice of ½ lemon
> 2 cups Very Brown Beef Stock
>    (see Index)
> 1 cup roasted red bell pepper,
>    cut into ½-inch strips
> Grated Fontinella cheese for
>    garnish

1. Preheat oven to 350°F. Roast eggplant, whole, on a cookie sheet for 45 minutes.

2. Remove eggplant from oven and, using heavy oven mitts, cut open and scoop hot pulp into blender container.

3. Add basil, garlic, salt, white pepper, and lemon juice to pulp in container and process on high until smooth, 2-3 minutes. Pour into 2-quart enameled soup pot with the beef stock and place over medium heat.

4. Stir in red peppers and let heat through, about 5 minutes. Serve with a generous helping of Fontinella cheese.

# LATE-HARVEST TOMATO SOUP

*Cherrill Cregar, a family friend, shares her recipe for a light, creamy-red tomato soup made with the fall harvest of plum tomatoes.*

Serves 4

2 tablespoons unsalted butter
  or olive oil
½ cup minced yellow onion
2 tablespoons all-purpose flour
1 quart chicken stock or
  Golden Garlic Broth (see
  Index), warmed
2 cups seeded and finely
  chopped very ripe plum
  tomato
Salt and freshly ground white
  pepper to taste
Minced fresh basil for garnish

1 Melt butter in a 2-quart nonreactive stockpot over low heat. Add onion and sauté until soft and translucent, about 10 minutes.

2 Sprinkle in flour and stir until onion and flour blend into a paste, about 3-5 minutes. Add heated stock gradually, stirring constantly. Bring to a simmer and thicken stock.

3 Mix in tomatoes, raise heat, and simmer, uncovered, until tomatoes are cooked, about 8 minutes. Season to taste. Serve hot with a sprinkling of basil.

# RICH HOT AND SOUR SOUP

*Forget your diet when you make this hearty meal-in-a-bowl soup. For the best results, place pork shoulder in the freezer for 30 minutes to semifreeze; it will be easier to cut the meat without shredding it. This recipe is based on a soup made by Pansy Luke at her Oriental Food Market and Cooking School in Chicago.*

Serves 8

1 ounce dried Chinese black mushrooms
½ ounce dried Chinese cloud ear mushrooms
1 ounce dried lily flowers
2 quarts Spicy Pork Stock or beef stock (see Index)
½ pound boneless pork shoulder, trimmed of visible fat
¼ pound bamboo shoots, chopped
½ pound firm tofu, cubed

1 teaspoon salt
1 tablespoon light soy sauce
2 tablespoons cornstarch
2 tablespoons water
1 large egg, beaten
½ cup rice vinegar
2 teaspoons finely ground white pepper
1 tablespoon dark sesame oil
1 tablespoon chili oil
½ cup very finely slivered scallion greens

1. Place the dried mushrooms and lily flowers in individual glass or ceramic bowls and cover with tepid water. Let soak while doing steps 2 and 3.

2. Pour stock into a large nonreactive stockpot and place over medium heat to simmer.

3. Trim pork shoulder and cut into narrow strips with a very sharp knife or cleaver. Add to stockpot along with chopped bamboo shoots.

80

4. Chop the softened mushrooms and lily flowers, after discarding the soaking water, and add to the pot. Stir in tofu and cook for 5 minutes.

5. Mix salt, soy sauce, cornstarch, and water until smooth; stir into pot and let soup thicken. Pour beaten egg into soup and wait a moment to let it solidify before stirring; the stirring action will break the egg into strands, like noodles.

6. Blend rice vinegar, white pepper, sesame oil, and chili oil in a tempered or warmed serving bowl. Pour soup over the hot oil, blend, and stir well. Sprinkle the scallion tops into the bowl and stir again. Serve immediately.

# ZUPPA VALDOSTANA

*Convito Italiano, a popular Italian food shop in Chicago, oper-
ates a small trattoria where spectacular soups are a house
specialty. Owner Nancy Barocci shares her recipe for baked
vegetable soup with fontina cheese. It's a great recipe for entertaining, because the soup may be "assembled" up to an hour
before serving.*

Serves 6

3 tablespoons unsalted butter
1 tablespoon olive oil
½ cup finely chopped yellow
  onion
¼ cup finely chopped celery
¼ cup finely chopped carrot
¾ pound zucchini, sliced into
  ¼-inch rounds (about 3
  cups)
1½ cups peeled, seeded, and
  chopped ripe tomato
1 tablespoon minced fresh
  parsley
1 tablespoon minced fresh
  basil

7 cups beef stock (see Index)
½ cup Arborio or Italian short-
  grain rice
1 cup shelled fresh or thawed
  frozen peas
6 slices dark bread such as
  whole wheat, dark rye, or
  black
½ pound fontina cheese,
  grated (approximately 1½
  cups)
⅓ cup grated Parmesan cheese

1. In a large Dutch oven, melt butter with olive oil over medium
   heat. Add onion, celery, and carrots and sauté for 3 minutes.
   Add zucchini, tomatoes, parsley, and basil and sauté for
   another 10 minutes.

2. Pour in beef stock and bring to a simmer. Add rice, cover and
   cook until rice is tender about 20-30 minutes. If you're using
   fresh peas, add them 5 minutes after adding rice; if you're
   using frozen, thaw them and add to soup 20 minutes after
   adding rice.

3 Preheat oven to 350°F. Butter one side of the bread slices and lay them, buttered side up, on a cookie sheet. Toast in the oven until crusty, about 10 minutes.

4 Pour soup into six warmed crocks. Divide grated fontina cheese into six equal portions. Sprinkle half of each portion over each soup bowl, top with a slice of bread, and sprinkle remaining fontina over bread. Top with a dusting of Parmesan cheese. (Crocks may be set aside at this point for up to 1 hour before baking.)

5 Raise oven temperature to 400°F. Place crocks in oven and bake for 20 minutes or until cheese is golden brown and bubbly. Serve immediately.

# SHERRIED MUSHROOM SOUP

*The Heartland Spa in Gilman, Illinois, serves ¾-cup portions of this soup to satisfy raging appetites with just 65 calories per serving.*

Serves 4-6

1½ teaspoons safflower oil
3 cups thinly sliced yellow
  onion
3 cups thinly sliced fresh
  mushrooms
3 tablespoons *fino* sherry
  (flamed to remove alcohol)
4½ cups vegetable stock (see
  Index)

3 tablespoons low-sodium
  tamari or soy sauce
1½ teaspoons cornstarch or
  potato starch
3 ounces skim milk
Freshly ground pepper to taste

1. Heat the oil in a 2-quart Dutch oven with a lid over medium-high heat. Add onions, stirring to cook evenly. Cook for 10 minutes or until golden.

2. Add mushrooms, reduce heat, and cover. Simmer, covered, for 5 minutes. Remove cover and cook until juices evaporate. Stir mixture often to make sure it doesn't stick.

3. Mix in sherry and stir. Add stock and tamari and bring to a simmer.

4. Blend starch into cold milk, whisking well to remove any lumps. Stir starch mixture into soup to thicken it. Season to taste with pepper and serve hot.

# SCALLOP AND POTATO CHOWDER

*The delicate flavor of scallops is bolstered by a dash of sherry in a creamy base of mashed potatoes.*

Serves 4

2½ cups milk or half-and-half
2 cups mashed russet or Idaho
   potatoes
⅓ cup *fino* sherry
¾ pound bay scallops, rinsed
   well
¼ cup minced chives or
   scallion greens
Salt and freshly ground pepper
   to taste

1. Place milk, potatoes, and sherry in a 2-quart saucepan over low heat. When milk base begins to simmer, fold in the scallops.

2. When just heated through and scallops are still tender, sprinkle soup with minced chives. Season to taste and serve in heated bowls with chowder crackers.

# MARKET BEAN SOUP

*Next time you go to a bulk market, buy any assortment of dry beans and make your own soup mix. For this recipe, from Pam Adrien Lyons, I blend 1 cup each of the following beans: adzuki, anasazi (turtle beans), black, great northern, kidney, navy, pink, pinto, red, and yellow split peas. You may want to blend other legumes or grains, such as barley, garbanzos, baby limas, black-eyed peas, green split peas, or lentils.*

*Mix the dried beans and keep them in an airtight canister. Before using, soak them in water mixed with a teaspoon of baking soda for 6–8 hours to reduce gas. It's easiest to set beans to soak in the morning, before going to work, for soup in the evening. A pressure cooker makes flavorful bean soup quickly; see the note at the end of the recipe if you would prefer to use one.*

Serves 6-8

2½ cups bean mix, washed and
    soaked for 6-8 hours in 2
    cups water and 1 teaspoon
    baking soda
3 quarts water
2 bay leaves
1 teaspoon dried marjoram
1 teaspoon dried thyme
1 28-ounce can crushed
    tomatoes

2 cups chopped yellow onion
1 tablespoon minced garlic
1½ cups chopped celery
½ cup chopped red bell pepper
1 teaspoon celery salt
Hot red pepper flakes to taste
3 skinless chicken thighs
1 pound cooked smoked
    turkey sausage
½ cup minced fresh parsley

1. Drain soaked beans and place in a large soup pot. Add water, bay leaves, marjoram, and thyme. Turn heat to low and simmer for 3 hours.

2. Add tomatoes, onions, garlic, celery, red bell pepper, seasonings, and chicken. Simmer for 1 hour. Remove and discard bay leaves. Remove chicken from pot, cut meat off bones, and return diced cooked meat to soup.

3 Slice turkey sausage and place in 9-inch skillet. Brown over medium heat and add to soup. Simmer for 5 minutes. Stir in parsley and serve immediately.

*Note: If you have a pressure cooker, you may cook the beans without soaking them:*

1 Place beans, seasonings, and 2 quarts water in a 6-quart pressure cooker. (The foaming action of beans during pressure cooking requires an extra-large pot.) Seal cooker according to manufacturer's instructions and bring to high pressure. Reduce heat and cook for 30–40 minutes. Reduce pressure quickly and test for tenderness. If beans are too chewy, add 1 cup water, seal, and cook for an extra 15 minutes at high pressure.

2 Reduce pressure and open cooker. Add 3 cups water and all remaining ingredients except parsley. Reseal and cook for 20 minutes at medium pressure. Reduce pressure quickly, remove chicken bones, dice chicken, and return cooked meat to pot. Adjust seasonings, add parsley, and serve.

# CIDER AND CHEESE SOUP

*Apples and cheese are natural partners, especially in this rich-tasting soup. Be forewarned that the tanginess of real cider cannot be duplicated with mere apple juice; plain juice is just too sweet.*

Serves 6

2 cups apple cider
1 quart chicken stock (see Index)
6 cups peeled, cored, and chopped apple (tart cooking apples such as Newtown Pippin or McIntosh)
2 cups chopped celery
1 cup nonfat dry milk

10 ounces low-fat, low-sodium Jarlsberg cheese, grated and allowed to come to room temperature (about 2½ cups)
½ cup chopped fresh parsley
½ cup grated fresh Parmesan
Salt and lemon pepper to taste
Apple rings for garnish

1. Mix cider and stock in a large enameled stockpot and add apples and celery. Cook over medium heat until tender, about 10 minutes.

2. In batches, puree soup in a blender to desired consistency (I puree about two-thirds, leaving some whole chunks of apple and celery for texture). Add nonfat dry milk to mixture while pureeing; return the creamy mixture to soup pot and set over low heat.

3. Slowly sprinkle cheese into soup, stirring often to prevent sticking and boiling, until cheese melts. Add parsley and Parmesan and season to taste. Garnish with sliced apple rings and serve hot.

# CURRIED ACORN SQUASH SOUP

*Fall brings small, tender acorn squash to market—try this recipe with young squash as well as the more mature winter acorn squash. The difference in texture and taste may surprise you.*

Serves 4

2 acorn squash (about 2 pounds total)
1 cup water
1 quart chicken stock (see Index)
¼ cup sugarless apricot fruit spread

2 tablespoons potato starch
3 tablespoons water
1 teaspoon curry powder
Salt and freshly ground pepper to taste
Toasted sesame seeds for garnish

1. Cut the acorn squash into quarters and remove seeds and stringy pith.

2. Place in a steamer basket in a large saucepan filled with 1 cup water; cover tightly and steam for 20 minutes or until tender. Remove from heat, reserving cooking liquid.

3. When squash has cooled enough to handle, remove skin. Cut cooked squash into chunks. Puree in a blender along with reserved cooking liquid.

4. Heat broth to a simmer in a 2-quart saucepan. Add squash and apricot spread.

5. Thin potato starch with 3 tablespoons water and slowly add mixture to soup, whisking constantly. Mix in seasonings and stir well to keep soup from becoming lumpy as it thickens.

6. Taste and add more curry powder or salt and pepper if needed. Serve hot with a sprinkling of toasted sesame seeds.

# CALVADOS CREAM OF SWEET POTATO

*A soup that is deceptively light in flavor while exceptionally filling. One guest at a dinner party remarked, "This could be dessert!"*

Serves 4-6

3 pounds whole, raw sweet
  potatoes
2 cups apple cider
1½ cups Very Brown Veal Stock
  (see Index)
3 tablespoons Calvados or
  applejack
1 tablespoon potato starch
  mixed with 1 tablespoon
  cold water if needed

1 teaspoon salt
Ground cinnamon or freshly
  grated nutmeg to taste or
  both
Sour cream or apple butter for
  garnish

1. Preheat the oven to 350°F and bake the sweet potatoes for 45 minutes. Scrape the potato out of the skins and puree in a blender along with ½ cup of the apple cider. You should have 4 cups of puree. (Alternately, peel and steam the sweet potatoes in a little water until tender, 20-25 minutes. However, the baked potatoes have a more concentrated flavor.)

2. Mix veal stock with remaining cider and Calvados in a 2-quart saucepan. Whisk in pureed potato, making sure there are no lumps. If the soup seems thin, add potato starch and whisk well. Simmer until thickened, about 15 minutes.

3. Ten minutes before serving, add salt and cinnamon and/or nutmeg to taste. Serve hot with a garnish of sour cream or apple butter.

# BUTTERNUT APPLE SOUP

*Meg Guthrie is a food writer based in Madison, Wisconsin, the home of a truly remarkable midwestern farmer's market. She uses the best of fall's harvest of apples and squash to make this soup.*

Serves 6

1 medium-sized butternut
   squash (about 2½-3 pounds)
6 McIntosh or Cortland apples
2½ cups fresh apple cider
2 cups half-and-half, or as needed

Peeled and grated fresh
   gingerroot to taste
Freshly grated nutmeg to
   taste, crème fraîche, and
   apple slices for garnish

1. Cut butternut squash into chunks and remove seeds and stringy pith. Place in the top of a vegetable steamer and steam over boiling water until tender, about 10-15 minutes. Remove from heat and let cool.

2. While squash cooks, peel, core, and chop the apples. Place in a 2-quart enameled saucepan and add the cider. Bring to a boil, reduce heat to a simmer, and let apples cook until they are mushy, about 15 minutes.

3. Scrape the squash from it skin. Discard the skin and place the squash in a food processor fitted with the steel blade. Puree until completely smooth. Scrape into a bowl.

4. Next, puree the apples and cider in the same food processor (you don't need to wash the bowl). Mix with squash in the enameled saucepan. Stir to blend well and heat just to a boil. Remove from heat.

5. Stir in half-and-half to the desired consistency. Add ginger to taste. Reheat, if necessary, before serving.

6. Garnish each serving with a light sprinkle of fresh grated nutmeg, a dollop of crème fraîche, and a few apple slices.

# CREAM OF WILD RICE SUPREME

*Indeed a supreme way to prepare wild rice—this soup, accented with pecans, goes well with duck, Cornish hen, and other game birds.*

Serves 4

1 cup wild rice
1 quart Very Brown Veal Stock
  (see Index)
1 cup water
Salt to taste
2 tablespoons butter
14 ounces fresh mushrooms,
  cleaned and sliced
1 cup chopped scallion
½ cup chopped shelled pecans
1½ cups milk or half-and-half
½ cup chopped fresh parsley
Freshly ground pepper to taste

1. Boil rice in stock and salted water in 3-quart soup pot until tender and fluffy, about 45 minutes.

2. Melt butter in a saucepan and sauté mushrooms over low heat for 5 minutes. Add scallions and pecan meats and stir.

3. Scrape mushrooms, scallions, and pecans into soup pot with rice. Add milk and parsley. For the best flavor, make ahead of time and reheat before serving. Season to taste with salt and pepper.

# HOT BORSCHT

*Almost all the late fall vegetables find their way into this borscht, which is good served with hot crusty whole-grain bread.*

Serves 6-8

3 cups peeled and sliced beets
1½ cups peeled and sliced
  carrot
1 cup diced celery
1½ cups diced yellow onion
½ cup peeled and sliced
  parsnip
1½ quarts Very Brown Beef
  Stock (see Index), heated

1 cup tomato puree
1 cup coarsely chopped green
  cabbage
2 cloves garlic, peeled and
  chopped
Salt and freshly ground pepper
  to taste
Sour cream and fresh or dried
  dill for garnish

1. Place beets, carrots, celery, onions, and parsnips in a 1-gallon soup pot and add hot beef stock. Simmer over medium heat for 20 minutes.

2. Add tomato puree and simmer for 10 minutes more.

3. Add cabbage and garlic and season to taste with salt and pepper. Cook for 15 minutes, making sure beets and cabbage are tender. Serve with a garnish of sour cream sprinkled with dill.

# CALDO DE RES

*El Taco Real, of Hammond, Indiana, draws crowds from Chicago and Michigan for its Mexican food. Ray Garcia shares his recipe for a traditional beef soup made with the last harvest of corn on the cob. Make it a day or 2 before serving to let the flavors meld.*

Serves 8

1 gallon water
2 cups chopped red onion
3 cloves garlic, peeled and
  chopped
6 pounds beef short ribs,
  trimmed and cut into 2-inch
  chunks
1 cup carrot, peeled and
  diagonally sliced into 1-inch
  chunks
1 cup diagonally sliced celery
  in 1-inch chunks
1 cup red bell pepper strips
1½ cups zucchini, sliced in ½-
  inch rounds

1½ cups 1-inch Idaho potato
  cubes
4 ears sweet corn, cut into 3-
  inch pieces
1 cup chopped cilantro leaves
2 cups green cabbage, sliced
  in ½-inch strips
2 cups seeded and chopped
  tomato
4 jalapeño peppers, seeded
  and sliced into thin strips
Salt and freshly ground pepper
  to taste
2 tablespoons tomato paste
  (optional)

1. In a 2-gallon soup pot, bring the water to a boil over high heat; add onion and garlic. Let it return to a boil; then add beef ribs. Bring to a boil, skim broth, and lower heat to a simmer. Cover and let simmer for 1½ hours or until beef is tender.

2 Add carrots, celery, and bell pepper and simmer, uncovered, for 20-30 minutes. Add zucchini, potatoes, corn, cilantro, cabbage, tomato, and jalapeño and simmer, uncovered, for 20 minutes more.

3 Taste and season as desired. If you want a deeper-colored stock, stir in 2 tablespoons tomato paste. Make this soup ahead of time and chill. The flavors will meld, and the extra fat may be skimmed off the top. Reheat over low flame and serve with corn tortillas and lemon wedges on the side.

# LEEK, POTATO, AND TOMATO SOUP

*A soup that only improves with age, this is good served with black rye bread.*

Serves 8-10

4 leeks
1½ cups chopped white onion
2 tablespoons olive oil
Salt and freshly ground pepper
   to taste
1 quart chicken stock (see
   Index)

5 cups peeled and diced
   potato (6 potatoes)
2 cups chopped fresh or
   canned tomatoes, drained
1 quart milk or half-and-half
2 tablespoons minced fresh
   parsley for garnish

1. Hold leeks at roots and slice lengthwise, keeping roots intact. Wash the leeks to remove grit (usually takes two or three rinses of fresh water). Drain and chop, using enough of the green tops to get a total of 5 cups.

2. Sauté onions and leeks in olive oil in a 12-inch skillet over medium heat for 10 minutes, adding salt and pepper to taste.

3. Bring stock to a boil in a large stockpot set over high heat. Add potatoes, reduce heat to medium, and simmer for 10-15 minutes. Add tomatoes along with onions and leeks. Simmer for 10-15 minutes more, or until vegetables are tender.

4. Warm milk in a 2-quart saucepan and add to stock mixture. Simmer until heated through. Serve hot, garnished with minced parsley.

# 5
# WINTER

Don't be dismayed by winter's seemingly mundane selection of produce. There are delights in every season's offerings, and winter is no exception. It's a challenge to the cook to make the most of the limited selection of produce by using ethnic seasonings to obtain different flavor profiles. Cope with winter by widening your view of what goes into the soup pot!

Beets, broccoli, all kinds of cabbages, celery, onions, potatoes, pumpkins, winter squashes, and yams are staples of the winter produce section. Greens, such as the curly-topped kale, are usually available too. All make fine additions to soups.

Try supplementing the seasonal selection with canned, frozen, and dried fruits and vegetables. Legumes make an appearance in many winter soups, with flavorful results. Exotic varieties of dried mushrooms, such as chanterelles, morels, and shiitake, may add a new dimension to plain soups. Unusual ingredients offer palates a respite from the typical winter's fare: an infusion of chicken soup and American ginseng is particularly restorative!

# PURPLE CABBAGE SOUP

*Be sure not to overcook the vegetables in this soup, or it will lose its appealing, vibrant colors—red cabbage actually turns purple as it cooks to tenderness, but develops a blue hue if it overcooks to mush.*

Serves 4

1½ quarts Very Brown Veal
  Stock (see Index)
1 teaspoon salt
1 teaspoon dried thyme
1 teaspoon caraway seeds
Hot red pepper flakes to taste
3 tablespoons tomato paste
4 cups cored and finely
  chopped red cabbage

2 cups small broccoli florets
2 tablespoons snipped fresh
  chives or minced scallion
  tops for garnish
Grated Parmesan cheese for
  serving

1. Place veal stock in a large soup pot over medium heat; stir in salt, thyme, caraway, pepper flakes, and tomato paste and bring to a simmer.

2. Add cabbage and broccoli; cook until just tender and still colorful, about 10-15 minutes. At this point, the red cabbage will quickly turn purple.

3. Ladle soup into bowls and garnish with chives or scallions. Pass a bowl of grated Parmesan cheese at the table.

# TRICOLOR CABBAGE SOUP

*When cabbage seems to dominate the produce section, make this aromatic soup for winter meals.*

Serves 6-8

1 large white onion, chopped
1 tablespoon minced garlic
2 tablespoons vegetable oil or margarine
1½ quarts Spicy Pork Stock (see Index)
1½ teaspoons dried dill
1 cup chopped bok choy
1 cup shredded red cabbage
1 cup shredded green cabbage

1 1-pound can tomatoes with juices, chopped
3 cups peeled and chopped white or Yukon Gold potato
2 tablespoons red wine vinegar
Salt and freshly ground pepper to taste

1. In a 9-inch skillet, sauté onion and garlic in oil or margarine over medium heat until tender, 5-6 minutes. Transfer them to a 3-quart stockpot and add stock, dill, bok choy, cabbages, tomatoes, and potatoes.

2. Over medium-high heat, cook until vegetables are tender, about 30-40 minutes. Season with vinegar and salt and pepper to taste.

# WINTRY CHICKEN SOUP

*Winter warmth can come from a blazing fire, a humming furnace, or a kettle of soup that simmers on a back burner of the stove. A good choice to fix on a winter weekend afternoon, this chicken soup cooks slowly, says its creator, Kristin Nelson.*

Serves 10

3 quarts water
1 5- to 6-pound chicken, cut up and skinned
4 cups chopped celery
4 cups chopped carrot
1½ teaspoons salt, or to taste
3 bay leaves, or to taste
1 teaspoon freshly ground pepper, or to taste
5 teaspoons low-sodium chicken bouillon granules

1 14-oz. can chopped no-salt tomatoes, drained
1 10-ounce package frozen peas
1 10-ounce package frozen corn
1 10-ounce package frozen green beans
1½ cups soup noodles *or* 1 cup white long-grain rice

1. Bring 2 cups of the water to a boil in a large stockpot. Add chicken and blanch 2-3 minutes to remove excess fat and unwanted by-products. Drain off water, leaving chicken in the pot, and add remaining 2½ quarts water. Bring to a boil.

2. Turn heat down to a simmer and add celery, carrots, seasonings, and bouillon. Cover, turn heat to medium, and cook for 20 minutes, stirring occasionally.

3. Add canned and frozen vegetables and noodles or rice. Turn heat to low and simmer for 20 minutes or until rice or noodles are cooked and vegetables are tender. Remove from heat and cool.

4. Remove chicken from pot and cut meat from bones. Chop meat into bite-sized pieces and return morsels to soup. For the best results, chill soup and remove fat before reheating to serve.

# ITALIAN CHICK-PEA STEW

*This soup is a lighter, more vibrant version of a favorite bean soup from Tuscany. It is particularly restorative on those wintry days when darkness falls early.*

Serves 4

1 cup dried chick-peas
1 quart water
1 quart chicken stock (see Index)
1 tablespoon olive oil
½ cup chopped yellow onion
3 cloves garlic, peeled and minced
1 red bell pepper, seeded and diced
1 green bell pepper, seeded and diced

1 1-pound can Italian plum tomatoes, drained
¼ teaspoon freshly ground white pepper, or more to taste
1 teaspoon dried oregano
Salt to taste
Grated Parmesan cheese *or* chopped fresh tomatoes and chopped fresh basil for garnish

1. Cover beans with water in a bowl and soak overnight. Alternately, place beans and water in pot, bring to a boil, boil for 5 minutes, and remove from heat; let pot stand for 1 hour before draining the beans. Reserve the bean liquid.

2. Place beans and 1 cup of their cooking liquid in a large stockpot. Add chicken stock. Bring to a simmer and cook for 1 hour or until beans are tender.

3. Pour olive oil into a medium-sized nonstick skillet and add onions and garlic. Sauté over low heat, stirring often, until soft and golden, 5–6 minutes. Add peppers, tomatoes, and seasonings and sauté for 5 minutes.

4. Add sautéed vegetables to beans in pot, stir well, and simmer to heat through. Season to taste with salt and pepper. Serve hot, garnished with Parmesan cheese or a spoonful of chopped fresh basil and tomatoes.

101

# SPICY YAM AND POTATO SOUP

*What to do when potatoes seem to be the only fresh vegetables you see? Combine them in a spicy, rich soup.*

Serves 4

4 cloves garlic, peeled and
  minced
1 teaspoon ground turmeric
1 teaspoon ground cumin
1 teaspoon hot paprika
2 tablespoons vegetable oil
1 pound yams, peeled and cut
  into ½-inch cubes
1 pound white potatoes,
  peeled and cut into ½-inch
  cubes

1 quart turkey or chicken
  stock (see Index)
Salt and freshly ground pepper
  to taste
⅓ cup chopped cilantro and
  Chili Croutons (recipe
  follows) for garnish

1. Sauté garlic and seasonings in oil in a 2-quart saucepan over very low heat until garlic is light gold (not browned).

2. Add yams and white potatoes and stir to coat with garlic and seasonings. Turn up flame to medium and sauté for 10 minutes.

3. Pour in stock and cook until potatoes are tender, about 20-25 minutes). Using a soup ladle, remove some of the potatoes and broth from the pot and place in a blender. Puree on high speed until smooth and return puree to soup pot.

4. Add salt and pepper to taste. To serve, garnish with cilantro and Chili Croutons.

# CHILI CROUTONS

3 tablespoons vegetable oil
2 teaspoons chili powder
2 slices white sandwich bread

Mix oil and chili powder and spread on both sides of bread. Cut bread into cubes and sauté in a nonstick pan over medium heat until bread is crisp and brown. Serve with soup.

# COLD CURE CHICKEN BROTH

*The peppers in this hot, hot broth will clear your head of a cold's congestion in minutes!*

Serves 4 (or 1 invalid's daily ration)

>  1 quart chicken stock (see
>    Index)
>  20 cloves garlic, peeled
>  5 sprigs fresh parsley, minced
>  6 sprigs cilantro, minced
>  ¼ cup fresh lemon juice
>  3 whole dried chilies
>  Lemon slices for garnish

1. Place all ingredients in a 2-quart enameled or nonreactive saucepan. Bring to a boil and then reduce heat and simmer, uncovered, for 30 minutes.

2. Pour the broth through a strainer. Drink hot, garnished with lemon slices, from a mug (and be sure to inhale the steam). May be diluted if necessary with additional plain chicken stock or hot water.

# TOM YAM KAI
## (THAI HOT AND SOUR CHICKEN SOUP)

*Banlu Vitayaudom owns the Pattaya Restaurant in Chicago; her version of Tom Yam Kai is incredibly simple to make. No lengthy simmering of stock is required; just use the cooking liquid from poaching the skinless chicken breasts.*

Serves 4

2 skinless, boneless chicken breasts, cut into strips 1½-inch long and ½-inch wide (total 14 ounces meat)
1 quart plus 1 cup water
3 slices dried galanga
½ cup lemon grass stalks in 1-inch pieces, crushed
3 kaffir lime leaves, dried or fresh
3 jalapeño peppers, cut into slivers

1 cup straw or button mushrooms, sliced in half
½ cup very thinly sliced white onion
3 tablespoons chopped cilantro
6 tablespoons nam pla (Thai fish sauce)
½ cup fresh lime juice
Cilantro sprigs *or* chopped scallions for garnish

1. Place sliced chicken breasts in a 2-quart saucepan and cover with the water. Add galanga and lemon grass and bring to a simmer for 10-15 minutes.

2. Add lime leaves, jalapeños, mushrooms, and onion to broth; stir well and simmer 5 minutes.

3. Add cilantro, nam pla, and lime juice. Warm through and serve immediately, garnished with cilantro or scallions. Caution: Lemon grass is tough and stringy—do not eat it, but set aside in your bowl.

*Note: Galanga, lemon grass, nam pla, and kaffir lime leaves are available at Thai grocery stores or by mail order (see Appendix).*

# PARTAN BREE

*Bree is the Scottish word for any liquid porridge or soup; here pieces of partan, or crab, float in an aromatic stock. I prefer to use Pacific Dungeness crab at its peak in the winter. Be sure to save the cooking liquid if you boil whole fresh crabs for the stock; otherwise, use a light fish or chicken broth.*

Serves 8

1 cup chopped yellow onion
1 cup diced celery
¼ cup oil
¼ cup all-purpose flour
2 tablespoons butter
2 cups skim milk
2 quarts water reserved from boiling crab *or* 1 quart fish or chicken stock (see Index) and 1 quart water

1 teaspoon freshly ground white pepper
1 teaspoon dried thyme
1 teaspoon dried basil
½ teaspoon grated lemon zest
2 pounds fresh crabmeat (see Note), cleaned, or thawed frozen crabmeat

1. In a large nonreactive Dutch oven, sauté the onions and celery in oil over low heat until soft, about 5 minutes. Remove vegetables with a slotted spoon and reserve.

2. Mix flour with additional butter and leftover oil in pot and cook to make a roux that is smooth, pasty, and golden brown. Use a whisk to remove any lumps. Whisk in the skim milk and cook until thickened, about 6-8 miutes. Stir to prevent sticking or lumping. Taste to make sure the raw flour flavor has disappeared. If not, cook for a few minutes longer. Return vegetables to pot and stir well.

3 Pour in crab stock or diluted chicken stock and seasonings; simmer until thickened slightly, about 10-12 minutes. Chop crabmeat and add to pot. Simmer for 5-10 minutes, until soup is warmed through and cooked but crab is still tender.

*Note: Expect to buy 5 pounds of whole king or Dungeness crab to obtain 2 pounds crabmeat. Try to buy crabs with big claws. Blanch crabs in 2½ quarts boiling water for 5 minutes; shells will change to a deeper color. Drain and reserve the cooking liquid. Let crabs cool and pry off top shells. Remove the inner gills, spines, and intestines. Ignore the green goo, also known as "crab butter." It is not harmful to eat, although it is salty.*

*Break the body in half and, using a nut pick or slender fondue fork, remove the meat from the shell sections. Crack the claws and extract the meat. Return empty claws and top shells to pot and boil for 15 minutes more. Strain and reserve for soup stock.*

# CREAM OF PEANUT SOUP

*Made in honor of my father, who adores the combination of bacon, peanut butter, and green onions.*

Serves 4

3 tablespoons unsalted butter or margarine
½-inch-thick slice yellow onion, peeled
3 tablespoons all-purpose flour
2 cups skim milk
2 cups chicken stock (see Index)
½ teaspoon celery salt

¼ teaspoon cayenne pepper
½ cup smooth peanut butter, or more to taste
4 slices bacon, cooked until very crisp and crumbled, and 1 scallion, including some green, chopped, for garnish

1. Melt butter in a 2-quart enameled pot set over low heat. Cook onion in butter until translucent, 10 minutes, remove and discard. Add flour to make a roux and cook until smooth, golden brown, and pasty, about 5 minutes.

2. Mix in skim milk, ½ cup at a time, using a whisk to make the mixture smooth. Raise heat and cook, stirring constantly, until thickened, approximately 5–8 minutes.

3. Pour in chicken stock, seasonings, and peanut butter. Heat through, about 10 minutes, stirring often to blend. Taste and adjust seasonings or add more peanut butter if you want a richer soup. Serve hot, garnished with crumbled bacon and scallion rings.

# WINTER SQUASH SOUP

*Here's a good way to warm up without fattening up—each cup of this velvety soup has just 70 calories.*

Serves 8

> 5 cups vegetable stock or
> Golden Garlic Broth (see
> Index)
> 1 cup diced yellow onion
> ¾ cup sliced celery
> ½ teaspoon dried sage
> 4 cups steamed and mashed
> winter squash (butternut or
> turban)
> 1 teaspoon ground coriander
> ½ teaspoon ground cumin
> 1½ tablespoons honey
> Chopped cilantro or celery
> leaves for garnish

1. Mix stock, onion, celery, and sage in a 3-quart soup pot. Bring to a boil and simmer for 20 minutes. Add all remaining ingredients except garnish, remove from heat, and let cool slightly. One-third at a time, puree stock mixture in a blender until smooth.

2. Return puree to soup pot and reheat. Serve hot, garnished with cilantro or celery leaves.

# THICK SPLIT PEA SOUP

*Made with carrot and lemon, this soup has both sweetness and fragrance; it also keeps for weeks in the refrigerator!*

Serves 6

3 cups green or yellow split
  peas
2 quarts water
1 cup roughly chopped carrot
½ cup roughly chopped yellow
  onion
1 clove garlic, peeled
1 bay leaf

2 thick lemon slices
1 teaspoon salt
½ teaspoon freshly ground
  white pepper
Sour cream or plain nonfat
  yogurt, with a little paprika
  or turmeric mixed in for
  color, for garnish

1 Wash and pick over split peas for grit. Place in a 3-quart nonreactive or enameled stockpot along with 7 cups of the water, carrots, onions, garlic, and bay leaf. Bring to a boil over medium heat. Skim off any foam; then reduce heat to very low and cover. Cook, stirring every 15 minutes or so, for 2-3 hours or until peas are very soft and puffy. Discard bay leaf.

2 Lift two-thirds of the cooked peas and all the cooked vegetables out of the pot and place in a blender. Puree on high speed with remaining 1 cup water until very smooth. Return puree to soup pot and add lemon slices, salt, and pepper. Let simmer over very low heat for 10-15 minutes more or until as lemony as desired. Remove lemon slices and serve hot, with sour cream or nonfat yogurt.

# POTATO AND ONION STEW

*This is a robust, satisfying soup for winter lunches made even heartier with bits of Canadian bacon. Add whole grain bread and salad to make it a full meal.*

Serves 6

2 tablespoons vegetable oil
4 slices Canadian bacon, slivered (about 5 ounces total)
1 pound mild Vidalia onions, peeled and cubed
3 pounds white boiling or redskin potatoes, peeled and cut into ½-inch cubes

1 quart potato broth (see Index)
½ cup grated carrot
2 teaspoons dried thyme
½ teaspoon salt
1 teaspoon freshly ground pepper
¼ cup chopped fresh parsley for garnish

1 Pour oil into a heavy 2-quart Dutch oven set over medium heat. Add bacon and stir to sauté; after 2-3 minutes, add onions and stir.

2 Add potatoes and stir. Cover, reduce heat, and let steam for 10 minutes. Pour in broth, carrot, and seasonings and stir; cover and let simmer for 30-35 minutes.

3 Uncover and raise heat; stir soup as it simmers vigorously. The potato and onions should be very soft. Garnish with parsley and serve immediately.

# SLOW-FIRE CHILI

*What gives this chili its slow fire is the addition of white pepper to the jalapeños, black pepper, cayenne, and garlic.*

Serves 6

2 pounds ground beef, preferably lean sirloin

5 cloves peeled and minced garlic

2 cups chopped white onion

3-5 tablespoons chili powder, to taste

3 jalapeño peppers, seeded and diced

1 teaspoon freshly ground white pepper

1 teaspoon cayenne pepper

1 teaspoon ground cinnamon

1 teaspoon freshly ground black pepper

1 cup chopped red bell pepper

1 cup chopped green bell pepper

3 cups fresh tomato puree *or* 1 28-ounce can tomato puree

4 cups seeded and chopped tomato *or* 1 28-ounce can tomatoes without salt, chopped

4 cups cooked or drained canned beans (try a blend of kidneys, pintos, anasazi, and black)

1 cup beer, preferably dark or bock beer, or more to taste

1. Cook beef in a 2-gallon soup pot over medium heat until juices and fat begin to simmer. Add garlic, onion, jalapeños, and seasonings and continue to simmer, stirring often, until beef is no longer red.

2. Add red and green bell peppers, tomato puree, chopped to-matoes, beans, and beer. Stir and simmer, uncovered, for 1 hour. Add more beer if you want a soupier chili; otherwise, this recipe should be pretty thick. Teetotalers may substitute beef or garlic stock for the beer. Taste and adjust seasonings. Serve over pieces of corn bread.

# WINTER KALE AND LENTIL SOUP

*Kale looks a little like an overgrown head of parsley, with very curly, lush green leaves that are a trove of vitamins A and C. This nutritious soup uses no meat stock, so it is very low in fat, too.*

Serves 4-6

1 pound red lentils
2 quarts vegetable stock (see Index) or water
2 cups chopped yellow onion
1 cup chopped celery
3 cloves garlic, crushed
1 teaspoon hot red pepper flakes

3 tablespoons tomato paste
2-3 tablespoons chopped cilantro, to taste
2 cups packed finely chopped kale leaves (see Note)
3 tablespoons fresh lemon juice
Salt and freshly ground pepper to taste

1. Wash and pick over the lentils. Place in a heavy 3-quart Dutch oven along with stock or water over medium-high heat and bring to a rapid boil. Skim off any foam or impurities and reduce heat.

2. When water settles to a slow simmer, add onion, celery, garlic, red pepper, and tomato paste, stirring well. Cover and cook until lentils are tender, about 30-45 minutes, depending on their size (red lentils cook faster than their green or brown counterparts).

3. Stir in cilantro, kale, and lemon juice, folding the curly leaves into the soup. Cook for 5-8 minutes, until the leaves are tender but not completely limp. Use the back of a wide wooden spoon to crush some of the lentils, making a thick, chunky soup. Taste and add salt and pepper if desired. Serve immediately.

*Note: Mature kale often has woody stems that run through the center of the leaves. Tear the greens away from any fibrous core when removing the stems.*

# SEATTLE SMOKED OYSTER STEW

*Trina Wellman, a chef in Seattle, Washington, shares her recipe for a savory stew. As a low-fat alternative, substitute milk for the half-and-half.*

Serves 4

3 tablespoons unsalted butter
½ cup diced yellow onion
½ cup diced celery
2 cups bottled clam juice
1½ cups half-and-half
1 pound smoked oysters,
    drained
2 tablespoons minced fresh
    parsley
1 tablespoon minced fresh
    chervil *or* 1 teaspoon dried
Freshly ground pepper to taste

1. Place butter in a soup kettle over medium heat. Sauté onion and celery in the butter until soft, about 5 minutes. Add the clam juice and half-and-half. Simmer for 10 minutes, but do not let boil.

2. Add oysters, parsley, and chervil and simmer for 2 minutes more. Season to taste with pepper and serve hot with oyster crackers.

# MUSHROOM VELVET SOUP

*A food processor for slicing mushrooms and a pressure cooker for simmering make preparation fast and simple; yet this soup can still be elegant enough for company. If you don't own a pressure cooker, see Note 1 at the end of this recipe for conventional-cooking directions.*

3 tablespoons vegetable oil
3 pounds mushrooms, cleaned, trimmed, and sliced thin
2 cups heavy cream
1 cup strong chicken stock (see Index)

1 tablespoon powdered dried shiitake mushrooms (see Note 2)
Salt and pepper to taste

☐1 Place oil in a 6-quart pressure cooker over medium heat. Sauté mushrooms for 10 minutes, stirring well, until they begin to soften.

☐2 Pour in cream, stock, and shiitake mushroom powder. Seal pressure cooker and cook, at second ring of pressure, for 20 minutes.

☐3 Remove pressure cooker from heat and cool contents rapidly by running cold water over top. When pressure is released, open lid. Stir soup and adjust seasonings.

☐4 Serve hot with crusty French bread.

*Note 1: To make this soup using conventional cookware, increase the amount of stock used to 2 cups, cook soup in an enameled 1-gallon pot with a tight-fitting lid, and increase the cooking time to 35–40 minutes over low heat. Be sure to keep the pot tightly covered while cooking.*

*Note 2: You can make your own shiitake mushroom powder by pulverizing four or five large dried shiitakes in a blender for 5–6 minutes. Scrape the powder out of the base and store in a tight-sealing, plastic container until ready to use.*

# WINTER GINSENG SOUP

*An infusion of ginseng is said to warm and energize the circu-latory system. Here ginseng and ginger are used to season cooked chicken and rice for a truly restorative soup.*

Serves 4

¾ pound skinless and
    boneless chicken breasts
6 dried shiitake mushrooms,
    soaked in water to cover
    until soft and then drained
    and chopped
1½ quarts water
½ cup rice
2 1-inch slices fresh
    gingerroot, peeled
1 ounce American ginseng
Salt and freshly ground pepper
    to taste
Chinese crispy noodles,
    crushed, for garnish

1 Place chicken, mushrooms, and water in a 3-quart soup pot and bring to a boil. Skim off any foam, reduce heat, and simmer for 15 minutes.

2 Add rice, gingerroot, and ginseng. Cook for 30 minutes at a low simmer. Remove chicken from pot, dice cooked meat, and add to soup. Add salt and pepper to taste. Serve warm, garnished with crushed Chinese crispy noodles.

# CHEDDAR AND CAULIFLOWER SOUP

*This is a variation on the traditional cheese-cauliflower soup enjoyed by so many northern Europeans. When properly handled, the cheese melts into a silky stock.*

*Cheese must be at room temperature before being added to the hot broth, or it will not melt. Should the cheese become tough and stringy (the result of adding it to a too-hot broth), use a slotted spoon to retrieve the cheese. Blend it with ⅓ cup cream in a blender on high speed until smooth. Slowly whisk the cooled cream-cheese mixture into the soup.*

Serves 6

3 tablespoons unsalted butter or olive oil
2 cups peeled carrot, sliced in ½-inch rounds
4 cups bite-sized cauliflower florets
1 cup chopped yellow onion

5 cups chicken stock (see Index)
½ cup nonfat dry milk
½ pound low-fat cheddar cheese, grated (about 2½ cups)

1. Melt butter or oil in a 3-quart stockpot over medium heat. Add carrots, cauliflower, and onions; sauté over medium heat until onions are soft and golden, about 10 minutes.

2. Pour in stock and milk powder, whisking well to dissolve the powdered milk. Reduce heat and simmer for 20 minutes. Turn off heat.

3. Ladle a little of the hot stock into a 2-cup measure and add grated cheese. Stir until cheese melts and then pour mixture into stockpot, stirring well. When cheese has melted into the soup, serve immediately with toasted bread on the side.

# Appendix
# MAIL-ORDER SOURCES

## ASIAN INGREDIENTS
(GINSENG, GALANGA, GINGER, MISO, ETC.)

DeWildt Imports, Inc.
Fox Gap Rd., RD3
Bangor, PA 18013
(800) 338-3433

Joyce Chen Unlimited
423 Great Road 2A
Acton, MA 01720
(508) 263-6922

Oriental Food Market
2801 W. Howard St.
Chicago, IL 60645
(312) 274-2826

## CHILIS AND HOT PEPPER SAUCES

Mo Hotta, Mo Betta
PO Box 4136
San Luis Obispo, CA 93403
(800) 462-3220

# BASES

Dean & DeLuca
Mail Order Dept.
560 Broadway
New York, NY 10012
(800) 221-7714

The Flavour Base
PO Box 2515
Dearborn, MI 48123
(313) 563-6870

The Heartland Trading Co.
2320 W. 110th St.
Chicago, IL 60643
(312) 779-5055

# FROZEN STOCKS

Perfect Addition
PO Box 8976
Newport Beach, CA 92658-
   8976
(714) 640-0220

# HERBS
## (INCLUDING FRESH WOODRUFF)

Caprilands Herb Farm
534 Silver St.
Coventry, CT 06238
(203) 742-7244

Indiana Botanical Gardens
PO Box 5
Hammond, IN 46325
(219) 931-2480

Taylor's Herb Gardens
1535 Lone Oak Rd.
Vista, CA 92084
(619) 727-3485

# INDIAN INGREDIENTS
## (CHUTNIES, CURRY POWDERS, RED LENTILS, ETC.)

Cinnabar Specialty Foods
214 Frontier Drive
Prescott, AZ 86303
(800) 824-4563

Patel Brothers
2542 W. Devon Ave.
Chicago, IL 60659
(312) 764-1857

# MUSHROOMS
## (FRESH MUSHROOMS)

Summerfield Farms
SR4, Box 195A-GC
Brightwood, VA 22715
(703) 948-3100

## (DRIED MUSHROOMS)

Chanterelles, button
  mushrooms, wood ears,
  cloud ears, morels, and
  more

Epicurean specialties
6817 California St.
San Francisco, CA 94121
(415) 668-1081

Woodland Pantry
Forest Foods
355 N. Ashland Ave.
Chicago, IL 60607
(312) 421-3676

# MEXICAN INGREDIENTS
## (ANCHO, JALAPEÑOS, AND OTHER CHILES)

Los Chileros de Nuevo Mexico
PO Box 6215
Santa Fe, NM 87502
(505) 471-6967

Santa Fe Seasons
624 Aguafria #2
Santa Fe, NM 87501
(505) 988-1515

# SEAFOOD
## (SMOKED OYSTERS, CRAWFISH, ETC.)

Crawfish, andouille sausage
  and Creole foods
French Market Seafood Co.
1101 N. Peters St.
New Orleans, LA 70116
(504) 522-8911

Pacific Northwest smoked
  oysters
Cascade Seafoods
PO Box 5221
Bellingham, WA 98227-5221
(206) 733-9090

## SHALLOTS

Mountain Meadow Farm
826 Ulrich Road
Prospect, OR 97536
(503) 560-3350

## THAI INGREDIENTS
(LEMON GRASS, GALANGA, KAFFIR LIME LEAVES, NAM PLA, ETC.)

Di-Ho Market
655 Pasquinelli
Westmont, IL
(708) 323-1664

Gourmet Treasure Hunters
10044 Adams Avenue, Ste.
305
Huntington Beach, CA 92646
(714) 964-3355

## VIDALIA ONIONS

Bland Farms
PO Box 506
Glennville, GA 30427-0506
(800) 843-2542

# INDEX

122

123

125

126